THE NEW RESTAURANT ENTREPRENEUR

AN INSIDE LOOK AT RESTAURANT DEAL-MAKING
AND OTHER TALES FROM THE CULINARY TRENCHES

KEP SWEENEY

Dearborn™
Trade Publishing
A **Kaplan Professional** Company

This publication is designed to provide accurate and authoritative information in regard to the subject matter covered. It is sold with the understanding that the publisher is not engaged in rendering legal, accounting, or other professional service. If legal advice or other expert assistance is required, the services of a competent professional person should be sought.

Vice President and Publisher: Cynthia A. Zigmund
Acquisitions Editor: Jonathan Malysiak
Senior Managing Editor: Jack Kiburz
Interior Design: Lucy Jenkins
Cover Design: Design Solutions
Typesetting: the dotted i

Published by Dearborn Trade Publishing
A Kaplan Professional Company

Printed in the United States of America

04   05   06   10   9   8   7   6   5   4   3   2   1

Library of Congress Cataloging-in-Publication Data

Sweeney, Kep.
    The new restaurant entrepreneur : an inside look at restaurant deal-making and other tales from the culinary trenches / by Kep Sweeney.
        p.   cm.
    Includes index.
    ISBN 0-7931-8567-X (6x9 pbk.)
    1. Restaurant management.   I. Title.
TX911.3.M27S93 2004
647.95'068—dc22

                                                                2004004599

Dearborn Trade books are available at special quantity discounts to use for sales promotions, employee premiums, or educational purposes. Please call our Special Sales Department to order or for more information at 800-245-2665, e-mail trade@dearborn.com, or write to Dearborn Trade Publishing, 30 South Wacker Drive, Suite 2500, Chicago, IL 60606-7481.

Dedication

To my beautiful wife, Alyse—the love of my life—and our two wonderful children, Madeleine and Connor

PART FOUR

Raising Capital

PART FIVE

Welcome to the World's Greatest Industry

The New Restaurant Entrepreneur is
the result of the convergence of my two related but different ca-
reers. I spent the first ten years of my working life in professional
kitchens. The three greatest influences in my culinary life were
my home, Jeremiah Tower, and Bob Kinkead. My mother is the
baker, and my father prepared all things savory. In my early years,
we rarely ate store-bought bread. On a Friday, my father would
bring home veal bones to prepare the base for Sunday night's dinner—French onion soup. My brother would prepare Peking duck
as an additional protein for Thanksgiving, and my friend from
two doors down would bring over a fresh lemon and a carton of
eggs for me to make a lemon soufflé for his after-school snack.

After college, I left for San Francisco to work for Jeremiah
Tower at Stars. Jeremiah was the hottest chef in the country at the
time, and I had never seen a cookbook like his New American Cuisine. During his book tour, I met him in Washington, D.C. I told
him that I had operated my own catering business in college and
wanted to work at Stars. Politely, he asked me to send him my ré-
sumé, and when he returned to San Francisco, he would review it
with his chefs. After months of hearing that Stars had no positions
available, I decided to move to San Francisco. The day I departed,
I sent Jeremiah a letter stating that I was moving to San Francisco
to work at Stars. I had no money and nowhere to live. Two months
later, after multiple interviews, I was hired at Stars as a prep cook
for $7.50 an hour. My responsibilities were simple: peel garlic and
tomatoes for eight hours a day.

Stars was a wonderful culinary experience. The menu was
written daily according to what was purchased that morning. I arrived at Stars every morning at 11 AM to help prep the exotic

dishes with the chefs before my shift. Then at 3 PM, the start of my shift, I began to peel garlic and make tomato concasse (crushed tomatoes) until 11 PM.

I worked my way up the ladder at Stars to the hot-food line and then left to work for Bob Kinkead at 21 Federal in Washington, D.C. The experience with Bob was the most meaningful of my culinary career. Bob is extremely creative. He took more chances than other chefs of his stature. He created dishes that were daring and fun.

After four years as a head chef of 21 Federal Nantucket, I decided it was time to open my own restaurant. I spent a few years losing money in Boulder, Colorado, so I began my second career by enrolling in the graduate school of business at the University of North Carolina to get an MBA. At that point my chef friends began looking to me for deal advice. I always got the same questions: How much of the restaurant do I have to give my investors? Do you think my investors would just give me a loan? Can I still get fired? Do the investors have any say in what I do with the business? In fact, I get those questions and questions like them every week. And those questions were the impetus for this book. I wanted to write a book that clearly outlined the process of a restaurant deal—a book that addressed concept development, deal structure, and lease negotiations.

I am often frustrated advising chefs. It isn't simply that restaurateurs aren't taught the skills outlined in this book, but, more fundamentally, many don't appreciate the need for these skills. I often witness a restaurateur or aspiring restaurateur sloppily expedite the capital raising, lease negotiating, and corporate development phase of the business. They believe they are so talented that they can make up any lost ground resulting from poor early stage preparation in operations. The fact is that when developing your restaurant, the outcome is foretold long before the restaurant opens. *Planning determines success.*

My MBA led to Salomon Brothers, where I was fortunate to be hired by a top Wall Street restaurant analyst. There I fine-tuned my financial skills; and through my work with the restaurant companies we covered, I was exposed to techniques in concept development, lease negotiations, and team building. I left Salomon Brothers to get back to my entrepreneurial life. At this point in my career I was armed with a strong understanding of both restaurant operations and finance. My life became project driven, and the projects were limited to restaurant-related enterprises. The range of opportunities was still surprisingly broad. I worked with ASPs (application service providers), online distributors, large restaurant companies, and start-up restaurants. I opened restaurants and developed concepts. I made money and I lost money. I have made a number of bad decisions and many good decisions. Throughout my career my greatest sense of pride is that each morning I wake up prepared for battle regardless of the prior day's results.

The New Restaurant Entrepreneur is composed of my stories and my experiences. The concepts I've included come from a combination of experience, working with smart people, and constant evaluation. It took me many years to develop my skills. Remember, there are no shortcuts. There is no easy path. According to restaurant industry statistics, the odds will be against you no matter how strong the plan. I believe that precise planning, fearless evaluation, and the ability to make hard decisions engineer risk out of your deal and make the outcome more predictable.

Six people who deserve special mention are:

My parents, Ginny and Leonard Sweeney, for encouraging me from a young age to take risks and not be afraid to fail.

Ken Wiles for being a great friend, ally, and advisor. Ken, particularly, in strategy, ethics, and finance heavily influenced many of the concepts introduced in this book.

David Housey for being the best writer I have ever worked with and for being a wonderful book partner.

Paul Westra for introducing me to the analytical side of the restaurant industry as well as believing in my entrepreneurial ventures.

Lisa Ekus for not loosing faith in this project and fighting for this book.

1

THE TRUE BEGINNING

Recognize what is truly important.

An entrepreneur encounters three distinct stages in developing a restaurant: Phase 1, the deal; Phase 2, the build-out; and Phase 3, operations. Phase 1 is strategic, whereas Phase 2 and Phase 3 are tactical. This book addresses Phase 1—the deal—which I consider the high-IQ phase. The fate of the business is determined here.

Phase 1 consists of four components: concept, team, real estate, and investors. In this phase we speak of menu engineering, energy sources, table-turns, and sales mix. We think about the difference in return on invested capital for sit-down lunch players versus upper-end casual-dining players. We discuss the benefits and drawbacks of discounting/couponing, and we position our concept using demand-side analysis.

In Phase 1, the entrepreneur addresses such questions as these:

- How much money do I need to raise?
- How much working capital do I need?
- How much equity do my investors require?

- Should my chef become a partner? How about the GM, the designer, the wallboard supplier?
- What should my concept be? Asian/hip? A steakhouse? A sit-down lunch restaurant?
- Should I select a concept that I am familiar with or a concept that is today's trend?

Typically, when we think of the restaurant industry we think of Phase 3, operations. By the time Phase 3 begins, the restaurant is either capitalized properly or it is not. The rent has already been determined. Management must live with the consequences of the real estate agreement. Those who plan poorly in Phase 1 and focus narrowly on Phase 3 are often relegated to operating a ridiculous, undercapitalized concept with an inexperienced team composed of lifelong underachievers.

It was in Phase 1 that Keith McNally created Balthazar, Wolfgang Puck created Spago, and Chris Sullivan developed Outback Steakhouse. These are well-thought-out restaurants where the concept is in concert with the team, the real estate, and the capitalization. My goal in this book is to help you better prepare your concept by sharing my experiences and insights. As Nobel Prize–winning physicist Niels Bohr once said: "An expert is a man who has made all the mistakes which can be made in a narrow field." You don't have to make them all; you can use some of mine.

SO YOU WANT TO OPEN A RESTAURANT?

2

KNOW YOUR SKILLS, USE YOUR SKILLS

Creating a restaurant is not time to learn; it's time to apply what you've already learned.

Phase 1 is best begun with a self-assessment. Once you decide to open a restaurant, you must design the concept. The four key questions to ask yourself:

1. What are you good at?
2. What do you like to do?
3. What is your background?
4. How do you spend your dining dollars?

You may think these questions don't apply to you. Perhaps you have previously opened a restaurant, are an executive at an established restaurant company, or have other reasons to exempt yourself. Identifying a market need is an achievement, and even experienced restaurateurs make costly errors by straying from their competencies. The restaurateur's best chance of success comes from focusing on his or her own background, experiences, and generation. In case you don't agree, I illustrate the importance of this personal assessment by way of examples. You will see that large, established restaurant companies and small, nimble entrepreneurs can both fail for ignoring these considerations.

THERE IS NO "TEAM" IN "I"

Back to the four questions. Understand that each question is directed to you. Take it personally. Do not answer using a team approach. It is not sufficient to say "my chef understands fine dining" or "my manager has operated nightclubs." If you intend to take the lead role, the president's role, you as an individual must fully understand the concept.

Let's say you are a sports fanatic and spend much of your leisure time in sports bars. You like beer and, oddly enough, can determine in a single bite whether the buffalo wings you ordered had been frozen. Why consider an investment in a different segment of the industry? Think how well you understand the guest at a sports bar. You inherently know what value is—you are your own guest. Further, you know the ideal product, hours of operation, entertainment component, and differentiation strategies. And you know whether your concept has a competitive advantage or is simply a "me-too" player.

I am amazed how often aspiring entrepreneurs develop a restaurant that they don't truly understand. They put themselves in a position to fail by developing the wrong concept. In so doing, they commit both a Type 1 error (taking a poor decision) and a Type 2 error (not taking a good decision). The point is not that these entrepreneurs don't belong in the restaurant business; the point is that they belong in the segment where they have unique insights. Mercifully, most of these restaurants never open because their creators don't have the track record required to raise capital.

Personally, I would like nothing more than to have a business venture to visit in Nebraska, particularly in football season. However, I have lived my entire adult life in the northeastern United

States and have little idea what a Nebraskan perceives as dining value. I would quickly fail in Omaha.

LARGE COMPANY FAILURES

I believe that Morton's Restaurant Group did not address the four questions before acquiring Bertolini's nor did the Carlson Group, the parent of T.G.I. Friday's, before developing Samba Room. Neither company understood what it was good at. Purchasing is the core competency of Morton's. Cooking certainly is not. Make the mistake of tasting one of its side dishes and you'll have ample proof of my assessment. For its part, Friday's excels at serving mediocre bar food to people who don't care for anything better. This company has no business owning, much less putting down, a white tablecloth. Yet it did just that with Samba Room.

Morton's

Morton's purchases and stores expensive inventory better than do any of its competitors. If you have a good dining experience at Morton's, it's because of the great raw materials. Its kitchen talent is quite ordinary. A few years ago Morton's acquired Bertolini's, a casual dining, moderately priced, Italian restaurant. Morton's is a high-end steakhouse with high average checks. Bertolini's requires a dramatically broader range of inventory as well as significantly more kitchen talent. I want to be clear here: Bertolini's is not a particularly good culinary experience, but executing its menu is much more difficult than executing Morton's menu. The acquisition of Bertolini's provided Morton's with many challenges. By not assessing its competencies at the outset, Morton's identified a skill mismatch only through trial and error. And Bertolini's was an error. Upper management's attention was diverted from projects that were consistent with Morton's competencies. Morton's has since divested most Bertolini's units at a discount.

Friday's

The Carlson Group made a fortune building and franchising T.G.I. Friday's, the ultimate after-work bar—a great place for jalapeño poppers and nachos. When I say "great place," I mean for people other than me. I have no use for the Friday's experience. This fact is not at all important to Carlson, nor should it be—I'm not the target customer. Where I *am* the target customer is where the food and service are designed to be noticeably above average.

The Carlson Group decided to open Samba Room and so expand vertically into fine dining. Samba Room is a high-end Latin restaurant that requires culinary and service precision. Whereas Friday's attracts low-level professionals looking to unwind after work with sugary cocktails and draft beer, Samba Room competes with the world's best restaurants. Friday's is no more likely to receive a serious food review than is a bowling alley. This too is unimportant to Friday's. It was, however, crucial to Samba Room, which was reviewed; no self-respecting reviewer would consider Samba Room a Douglas Rodriguez concept—even though it is!

I wonder how the creators of Friday's could have ever expected to compete with the best restaurants and restaurateurs in the country. Reviews are as important to restaurants as they are to movies. In short, although well capitalized, the Carlson Group's vertical expansion was a failure long before Carlson opened the first Samba Room.

THE TEAM APPROACH

In 2002, I was hired as a menu consultant for a restaurant project in Manhattan. One of the two operating partners was a high-end lounge manager and the other was a contractor. Their concept was a three-star Latin American restaurant that would convert late night into a lively bar scene. The food and service were to be among the finest in the city. Further, the restaurant would operate 24 hours a day in an industrial area of Manhattan with little foot traffic. The restaurant would produce high-quality breakfast, lunch, dinner, and late-night food as well as offer off-premise catering and delivery. The partners did not fully appreciate the difficulties of launching this project. Neither of them had ever worked in a three-star restaurant, and only one Manhattan Latin American restaurant had ever received a three-star rating.

Because they had no experience with food or service of this quality, the operating partners had to outsource a good deal of the decision making. They were, in effect, operating partners in name only; that is, they couldn't contribute to menu development, service standards, or any aspect of operations. Because they lacked expertise in business, marketing, and raising capital, they had to rely on a brigade of consultants and minority partners to fulfill their idea. In concept development, God is in the details. The nuances are critical to success. Without an experienced expert as president, a three-star Latin American restaurant with a late-night bar scene and catering and delivery is a fanciful imagining, not a restaurant concept.

THE BRIGADE

The operating partners had to outsource nearly every functional element of the enterprise. They made a former investment banker a partner to handle the business end. Access to the elite crowds in New York was required, so a marketing partner was brought in. Both people performed admirably and the investment was raised.

Although the project was funded, the concept lacked both a menu and production systems. Shortly after my engagement as menu consultant, the operating partners interviewed bar consultants. They needed help in developing a drinks menu as well as wine and spirits programs. In the event you are trying to keep count, this small restaurant in a low-traffic area of Manhattan had two operating partners, one business partner, one marketing partner, one culinary consultant, and one identified, but not engaged, bar consultant. At this point, even with optimistic projections, labor costs plus payroll taxes exceeded 50 percent of sales. Even so, the operating partners weren't finished—they went on in search of a general manager and a dining room manager.

Incidentally, I agreed with their reasoning on each individual hire. Should they handle business affairs? No. Should they direct marketing? No. Should they lead capital raising? No. Should they write a Latin food menu? No. Should they create a Latin drinks menu? No. Should they design service? No.

What *should* they do? In this instance, the question was what could they do. The frank answer was "not enough." They recognized some of their own weaknesses but didn't have sufficient vision to hire complementary support.

Confusion was on every level. I developed a total of eight menus attempting to determine who management believed would be the customer. The menus were vastly different. Two of the menus are presented for comparison and discussion (see Figures 2.1, 2.2, 2.3, and 2.4).

Each menu provided a different consumer experience. However, management could not understand how each menu was designed to serve a distinct occasion. How can you expect to run a hot New York Latin restaurant when you cannot recognize the differences in two menus? The casual-dining menus have multiple menu categories allowing for multiple dining occasions. Guests may elect to get coffee and dessert, a snack, or a full meal. The casual-dining menus used recognizable and relatively inexpensive ingredients. The upper-end casual-dining menus focused the guest experience on tapas that used exotic ingredients. Most of the upper-end casual-dining menus offer complex plates with multiple ingredients and more difficult techniques than do the casual-dining menus. Menu perception is the result of the city where the restaurant is located. The casual-dining menus could be featured in a top restaurant in all but a few U.S. cities. Both of

FIGURE 2.1 Casual-Dining Latin Menu Page 1—Estimated Zero Star

LATIN

Pizzas

Mushrooms, sweet onion jam, manchego cheese & almonds
Chorizo & ham w' queso fresco, tomatoes & black olives
Vegetable tossed in garlic & olive oil topped w' queso fresco
Oven-dried tomato w' manchego cheese, queso fresco
& crispy garlic

Tapas

Selection of Cured Meats - Serrano ham, Spanish salamis & chorizo
Selection of Spanish Cheeses - Cabrales, Manchego, Mahon
Almejas a la marinara (Clams cooked w' wine, chorizo & tomato)
Calamares a la romana (Deep-fried squid)
Pulpo a la Leonesa (Octopus w' sweet onions & balsamic)
Gambas al ajillo (Shrimp w' garlic)
Salpicon de mariscos (Spicy seafood parfait w' avocado)
Albondigas con salsa de tomate (Meatballs in tomato sauce)
Pinchos morunos (Beef kabob w' Cabrales cheese)

Starters

Sopas
Black bean soup
Sopa del día (soup of the day)

Empanadas
Chicken w' ancho & onion
Beef w' raisins & pepitas
Shrimp w' mango & coconut

Salads

Shrimp w' mango, avocado & roasted peppers
Chicken, Cabrales blue cheese & Serrano ham on crispy lettuce
Escalivada - marinated eggplant, peppers & tomatoes
Asparagus w' a saffron mayonnaise

FIGURE 2.2 Casual-Dining Latin Menu Page 2—Estimated Zero Star

Main Course

Sandwiches
(served w' a choice of yucca fries or tostones)
Cuban - Slow roasted pork, ham, pickles & mustard
Chicken - slow cooked in chiplote & orange w' avocado
Steak w' caramelized onions, ancho mayo & queso fresco
Grilled shrimp - shrimp, peppers & oven-dried tomatoes
Grilled manchego cheese w' oven-dried tomatoes
Hamburger - ½ pound burger served w' manchego cheese

Entreés
Breast of chicken w' saffron & olive rice topped w' red mole
Grilled snapper on a bed of coconut-chili rice w' salsa verde
Pepita crusted loin of pork w' avocado salsa & tostones
Pot of Zarezula stew w' clams, mussels, shrimp & snapper
Grilled sirloin steak w' yucca fries & chimichurri sauce

Side Dishes
Yucca fries
Tostones
Black beans & rice
Grilled corn w' chili aioli
Potato & ham croquettes

The Ending

Sweets
Rice pudding
Flan
Churros w' hot chocolate
Warm chocolate chip,
coconut & cashew cookies

Café y chocolate
Café con leche
Spanish coffee - regular
& decaf
Espresso - regular & decaf
Cappuccino - regular & decaf
Hot chocolate w' chili

FIGURE 2.3 Upper-End Casual-Dining Latin Menu Page 1—Estimated One Star

---

LATIN

SOUPS

Zarzuela   6

*Composed of a selection of fish & shellfish w' toasted nuts
and a hint of saffron in a tomato broth*

Black Bean

Creamy black beans served w' sour cream & salsa

TAPAS/CEVICHE/RAW BAR

Tuna Cerviche   8

Sushi-quality tuna marinated in wasabi, cucumber, seaweed & sesame

Shrimp & Scallop Ceviche   7

Fresh bay scallops and gulf shrimp tossed w' tangerine, avocado & mint

Striped Bass Ceviche   7

Marinated w' roasted garlic, tomatillo & cilantro

Topless Oysters   2 ea.

Chilled oysters on the half shell topped w' mojito mignonette

Garlic Steamed Clams & Mussels   8

*Cockles & Prince Edward Island mussels steamed w' garlic, orange,
tomato & white wine*

Calamari   6

*Grilled calamari stuffed w' braised beef served
w' a tomato-garlic sauce*

Ham Croquettes   6

Crispy ham and potato fritters served with a spicy mustard dipping sauce

(continued)

FIGURE 2.3 *Continued*

Ropa Vieja   8

"Old clothes" & sweet & sour cabbage served in a crispy wrap
w' a raisin & balsamic dipping sauce

Chicken Wings   7

Crispy chicken wings tossed in guava glaze served
w' vanilla-black pepper dipping sauce

Spare Ribs   9

Slow cooked spare ribs in a mango glaze

Steamed Vegetables   6

Selection of market vegetables served in a bamboo steam basket
w' two dipping sauces

Chili Relleno   9

Tempura battered roasted Cubano chili stuffed w' garlic, onion, cilantro,
cheese & lime

Grilled Sardines   9

Served w' a citrus relish

Selection of Cured Meats   9

Serrano ham, Spanish salamis & chorizo served w' croutons
& fig marmalade

Selection of Spanish Cheeses   9

Valdeon – sharp, creamy, blue; Manchego – hard, creamy;
Mahon – sharp, firm

FIGURE 2.4 Upper-End Casual-Dining Latin Menu Page 2—Estimated One Star

LATIN

<u>SALADS</u>

Garden Tomato Salad   10

*Garden tomato tossed w' cucumber, avocado, Manchego cheese
& lime vinaigrette*

Grilled Vegetable Salad   10

*Served with eggplant, zucchini, peppers, tomato
& almond crusted goat cheese*

Crab   12

*Crunchy lettuce w' Maine crab, mango, avocado, tomato,
& yellow peppers*

<u>FLATBREADS</u>

Clam   10

Topped w' clams, chorizo, white cheese, garlic slivers & cilantro

Steak   12

*Topped w' Ropa Vieja, sweet onion jam, mushrooms,
Manchego cheese & almonds*

Vegetable   8

*Selection of marketed vegetables tossed in garlic & olive oil
and topped with two cheeses*

(continued)

FIGURE 2.4 *Continued*

ENTRÉES

Grilled Breast of Chicken
Served w' Creole-style fricassee of mushrooms, crayfish,
fingerling potatoes & artichokes

Salmon
Grilled filet mignon of salmon in a corn-chili ragout w' potato puree
& cilantro oil

Roasted Loin of Pork
Served w' slow cooked potato puree, frisee & orange salad
& an ancho orange sauce w' grilled chorizo

Roasted Cod
Wrapped in Serrano ham served w' brandade potato puree
& spinach & sweet garlic

Grilled Tenderloin of Beef
Served w' a Picon cheese & roasted shallot crust, crispy fries
& a side of chimichurri sauce

SWEETS   6

Rice Pudding Crème Brulee
Vanilla Flan w' Pineapple
Valrona Chocolate Fondue
Valrona Chocolate Milk Shake

these menus were designed for the highly sophisticated New York market.

Without a comprehensive and unified vision of the project, the kitchen menu could not be in harmony with the bar menu, the décor, the ambiance, the marketing program, or, most critical, the budget. As the proverb warned, "Too many cooks spoil the broth."

Ten months later, the project had still not reached the stage where the founders' skills were valuable. One partner has tremendous experience in high-end nightlife. He has managed a few of the more famous lounges and dance clubs in the country and has a reputation for hiring and retaining great staff. Why didn't he develop his first entrepreneurial venture around his skills and background? Why compete in a segment of the market about which you are unfamiliar? In the early years of your entrepreneurial life, give yourself the greatest chance of success by sticking to your background and your generation.

Why would the two operating partners proceed as they did? Were they mentally ill? Did they have self-destructive personalities? No and no. Quite simply, they indulged a dream that was more folly than business. This tale ends as 95 percent of all restaurant ventures do—in failure. The investor lost faith in the team. Most of those hired were fired, and the investor replaced the concept and the management team in an effort to get his money back. The operating partners had asked themselves the four questions, but they didn't apply them personally.

3

DEMAND-SIDE ANALYSIS VERSUS SUPPLY-SIDE ANALYSIS

Think how you use restaurants.

Today, the economies of scale for chain restaurants is so great that independent restaurateurs must be both careful and savvy to withstand the competition. Understanding skills is a critical step; however, skills can be manifest in many ways. The entrepreneur employs his abilities according to his assessment of the marketplace.

Entrepreneurs can adopt a supply-side approach or a demand-side approach to analyze their competitive universe. A supply-side approach segments the industry by format or menu. For instance, a steakhouse competes with a steakhouse and a fast-food chicken restaurant competes with other fast-food chicken restaurants. I prefer to segment the industry from the demand side—that is, by the way customers use the restaurant. A demand-side approach segments the industry by dining occasion. Consumers make eating decisions on the basis of check average and desired experience. For instance, Morton's competes with steakhouses and fish houses alike, provided that each offers a similar experience at a comparable price.

I often have conversations with restaurateurs concerning a concept's viability. The restaurateurs may argue that they will have no competition because they will have the only restaurant offering a particular cuisine at particular price points. I was told many times in graduate business school that I should open a restaurant in Chapel Hill, North Carolina. A colleague would comment that perhaps a pasta restaurant would be successful because there are no pasta restaurants in Chapel Hill. After further conversation, it became clear that my colleague meant a high-end pasta restaurant. Again, because guests dine by occasion, not by cuisine, a high-end pasta restaurant may compete with a steakhouse. Further, a Guatemalan papusa bar would certainly be unique in Lincoln, Nebraska, but the truth is that this niche doesn't exist. Again, competition is not determined by cuisine. Cuisine can be a differentiating characteristic, but a concept's competitive universe is based on the experience provided. The experience is composed, among other factors, of food, décor, time commitment, menu price, service, and location.

Damon's International retained me to complete a repositioning study. Management wanted to determine the differentiating characteristics of price and menu between upper-end casual-dining restaurants (like Outback Steakhouse and The Cheesecake Factory) and casual-dining players (like Damon's and Chili's). To view Damon's competition using the supply-side technique would create a competitive universe of rib-focused dining establishments. A supply-side view would determine that in a market without a barbeque restaurant, Damon's was without competition. In reality, Damon's competition is any restaurant that competes in casual dining. Most clever analysts segment the industry into four categories:

1. Fast food
2. Family dining
3. Casual dining
4. Premium dining

Each category competes within its category. Fast-food competitors like McDonald's, Arthur Treacher's, and Arby's compete on price points, location, and speed of service. Family-dining competitors like Bob Evans, Cracker Barrel, and Buffets compete on price points, location, and quality. Casual-dining competitors like Applebee's, Damon's, and Olive Garden compete on price points, location, and quality. In premium dining, guests select from P.F. Chang's, The Cheesecake Factory, and Outback Steakhouse, whose concepts compete on price points, location, quality, and distinctiveness of the experience. In short, Damon's competes with casual-dining restaurants and not with other restaurants that feature ribs.

EXAMPLE

A few years ago, my consultancy worked with an online home-meal replacement company. The company was a branded specialty retailer of quality foods and meal solutions with a physical store and a Web interface. Through its unique "click-and-mortar" approach, the company intended to launch a national brand and consolidate the fragmented home-meal replacement market by satisfying its customers' demand for a total meal solution—better food than customers can make for themselves combined with the convenience of takeout and delivery.

This concept was unique in its format. Supply-side analysis would have concluded that the company was without peer and could "own" its niche. Our competitive analysis illustrates the fundamentals of demand-side analysis, which is critically different, especially in its conclusion.

SUPPLY-SIDE ANALYSIS

We determined that all sectors of the restaurant and grocery industries are reacting to America's need for meal solutions. A supply-side approach looks at the competitive environment from the standpoint of where consumers can satisfy their need for prepared meals. Figure 3.1 identifies the meal suppliers that would be competition for our company.

A supply-side approach would suggest that my wife and I would first decide we wanted to eat seafood and then we wanted to eat out, so we would be essentially indifferent about choosing among providers. However, not all seafood restaurants are alike. You have the culinarily horrendous Joe's Crab Shack (however, a great playground for kids) or the wonderful Aqua at the Bellagio. Although both restaurants use consumers' disposable income, they are not in the same competitive universe. As consumers, we are not indifferent.

FIGURE 3.1 Home-Meal Replacement—Supply-Side Analysis

Grocery stores	For years, the grocery industry has attempted to penetrate the lucrative home-meal replacement sector (HMR). Poor food quality and the perception of factory food limit the opportunity of this sector.
Food/Meals e-tailing	A classic supply-side response: The ability to prepare, package, and ship a high-quality meal does not adequately address the principal need in the marketplace, namely convenience. The principal drivers of this segment are curiosity and novelty.
Last-mile delivery companies	Takeout Taxi has failed to deliver quality to consumers. It does not control the most critical point of its value chain: food production and packaging. Its suppliers are restaurants that treat delivery as a noncore business and are therefore less critical than are sit-down restaurants. Kozmo will never convince diners to order meals where they order videos and DVD players. Similarly, Webvan carries a wide range of SKUs (stock-keeping units) of commodity products. Internet-based grocers have perception and execution problems with home-meal replacement.
Restaurants	Companies such as Outback Steakhouse are retrofitting their units to accommodate a pickup program. Though supply-side driven, these functionalities are well received by consumers.

DEMAND-SIDE ANALYSIS

We first segmented market demand according to product use and occasion. Further, our demand-side analysis identified critical success factors. Figure 3.2 identities the four user groups within the home-meal replacement market: on the run, eat at home, gourmet foodie, and health conscious. The figure outlines consumer psychographics, critical success factors, and the traditional channels through which consumers generally purchase their meals.

We found that in producing a scenario analysis for each group, we could better understand the four consumer groups.

DEMAND OCCASIONS SCENARIO ANALYSIS

On the Run

Susan is a tax attorney. Her work schedule is unpredictable and demands personal flexibility. She would have considerable difficulty preparing a meal even if she were inclined to do so. Her husband, Brandon, offers few solutions to their meal issues because of his professional commitments. The couple try to speak by telephone in the early afternoon to assess the prospects for the evening. Sometimes they reward themselves with a nice dinner out. Other times, they consider the time commitment of a good restaurant experience to be a sacrifice. Relaxing at home is the reward they crave. The best case for this couple is to have their restaurant-quality meal at home. What are the characteristics of a meal solution they would devise for themselves?

- Convenience/Speed
- Restaurant quality
- Ease of preparation/cleanup

FIGURE 3.2 Demand Occasion Analysis Table

DEMAND OCCASION	CONSUMER PSYCHO-GRAPHICS	FOOD CHOICES	CRITICAL SUCCESS FACTORS	TRADITIONAL CHANNELS
On the run—Demand for option to eat in or take out, kid-friendly environment (home), convenient location, fast service	Value conscious, no menu planning, less health conscious, not a foodie	Pizza, chicken, burgers, Chinese, Mexican	Quality/ Freshness ✓ Branding Variety Concept ✓ Packaging ✓ Price ✓ Speed	Fast-food chains, delis, cafes, bakeries, local limited-service restaurants, local full-service casual dining restaurants
Eat at home—Demand for: easy preparation, low cost, great taste, quick cleanup, variety for everyone through the week	Somewhat health conscious, time starved, value conscious, families, young singles, tired	Chicken stews, salads, steak, pasta	✓ Quality/ Freshness Branding ✓ Variety Concept Packaging ✓ Price ✓ Speed	Supermarkets, convenience stores, television, Internet, local take-out delis
Gourmet foodie—Demand for: recipes difficult to make at home, ethnic foods, seasonal products, imported goods	Serious home cooks with no time, entertaining shuns imitation, experiments with food	Full entrées with accompaniments, complex sauces, wine, desserts	✓ Quality/ Freshness ✓ Branding ✓ Variety ✓ Concept ✓ Packaging Price Speed	Specialty food stores, fine-dining restaurants, high-quality boutiques
Health conscious—Demand for: low-fat foods, freshness, organic, seasonal products	Values convenience, time starved, young families, young singles, would rather cook if had the time	Salads, seafood, sports foods	✓ Quality/ Freshness Branding ✓ Variety ✓ Concept Packaging Price Speed	Specialty food stores, natural food delis, supermarkets greenmarkets

Eat at Home

Andy recently moved to New York from Illinois. Although he was raised on home-prepared meals, he never learned to cook. He misses the variety and convenience afforded him when he lived at home but doesn't intend to ever put much effort into meal preparation. For his first several postcollegiate years, he was content with pizza and pad Thai as his meal staples. Since arriving in New York, he has been exposed to many types of dishes and has found his tastes are broader than those of his parents. Furthermore, he is image conscious and believes that a successful person does not live in an apartment littered with take-out menus and Chinese food cartons. This is what he wants at mealtime:

- Convenience/Speed
- Image/Branding
- Variety

Gourmet Foodie

Mike is a national accounts representative. His duties require him to travel several times each month. His job is demanding, and even when working from his home, he seldom thinks about eating until hunger sets in. Marne, Mike's wife, is rather accomplished in the kitchen. She likes to plan and host dinners as a social activity. Since their daughter began school, though, Marne has returned to her job at the bank. Although cooking is a hobby for both of them, this activity waits for the weekend. Having grown accustomed to high-quality meals, they are loath to compromise during the week. These are their principal meal solution demands:

- Convenience/Speed
- High quality
- A child-friendly option

Health Conscious

Ever since Jim has been dating Adriana, he has been quite health conscious. She has always worked out and watched what she's eaten. She tells Jim that the best compensation for working hard is feeling good, not bingeing. Having been together several months, they have collectively agreed to indulge occasionally but maintain a healthful diet as a rule. Come dinnertime they would be best served by:

- Convenience/Speed
- Healthfulness
- Variety

CONCLUSION

The two types of analyses yield very different conclusions. I think our own experience supports the wisdom of demand analysis. In my own life, when my wife and I decide to go out to dinner, the key determinant is price. For example, we may decide to go for a causal dinner where our options include Chinese food, pizza, or burgers. Alternately we may elect to celebrate and choose between a steakhouse and a celebrity-chef-driven restaurant.

Demand-side analysis is more difficult to perform than supply-side analysis but is infinitely more useful. The customer's thought process is not complex with regard to a dining decision. However, influencing this decision making requires the insight derived from profound analysis and hard work. Either that or luck.

4

TARGET MARKET

Understand buying before selling.

There are two ways to develop a restaurant concept: the what-you-can-provide approach (supply) or the what-they-want approach (demand). A restaurant company *must* take the demand approach. The demand approach is particularly important to restaurants because of the large number of competitors in the industry and the unlikelihood of a revolutionary restaurant product. The supply approach is almost bound to fail. The goal in the demand approach is to directly satisfy guests' needs by knowing them. Both history and logic tell me that new entrepreneurs will be most successful by targeting their own generation and socioeconomic group. All of us know what we like and what our friends like. We know what our peer group perceives as value. Knowing your customer is critical to success, so why not begin with a customer you already understand? Try to determine what the market needs and try to penetrate a specific niche.

Who is your target market? Your success is predicated on precisely answering this question. Most privately owned restaurant companies don't know who their customer is. This lack of awareness tends to be the case whether or not the restaurant is successful. Success is often luck. A restaurant just happened to open in a location that was heavily populated with the restaurant's target customer, and the offerings happened to be coveted by the target guest. Luck can work once, but luck is not duplicative. A complete target market analysis will engineer out a great deal of an entrepreneur's risk. It will answer questions about pricing, hours of operation, location, décor, service, and menu offering. A poorly defined target market results in muddled operations, confused guests, lack of brand equity, and failure.

Most entrepreneurs find this analysis too tedious and define their target market broadly and, therefore, ineffectively. I generally read statements in business plans like "Our concept will target upscale urban 25- to 55-year-olds." What does that mean? Answer: It means nothing. It provides no strategic guidance to the business. To begin with, the words *upscale* and *urban* have meanings in New York different from those in Los Angeles. In New York, upscale urbans live in apartments and travel to your venue in a taxi or by car service. In Los Angeles, an upscale urban patron will most likely live in a house and drive to your restaurant in his or her own car. Therefore, in New York the marketing plan and the amenities will be significantly different from those in Los Angeles. For instance, you'll select different distribution channels. In Los Angeles, a radio ad will be more effective than it will in New York because New Yorkers spend less time in cars. In New York, a promotion with a car service and a limousine company will be more effective than it will be in Los Angeles. Car service is a way of life with upscale New Yorkers and not only for special occasions.

To continue, an upscale 25-year-old and an upscale 55-year-old have very different needs, tastes, and experiences. It is difficult to direct a marketing plan to both groups, and further, it is impossible to craft services and amenities that appeal to both groups. Look at table spacing. A 25-year-old generally likes to dine in an upbeat atmosphere, is willing to talk over music, and likes to trade table space for a lower check. Most upscale 55-year-olds aren't willing to trade table space for a lower check and have no interest in talking over loud music.

Let's look at steakhouses. Morton's, Ruth's Chris, and Fleming's have similar price points and menus, but their target markets are very different. Morton's believes that its core guest is a male executive. It designs its stores to look like private men's clubs. Generally, Morton's does not have windows, has little signage, and has one solid wood front door. The public should conclude that this restaurant is not for everyone but only for the successful. Ruth's Chris is more welcoming than Morton's. Ruth's Chris is designed to have a broader appeal—not specifically businesspeople. Consequently, Ruth's Chris may locate in a strip mall or a window-filled storefront. I find Fleming's the most interesting of the three examples. It offers a sexier steak environment. When you walk into a Fleming's, you'll immediately notice younger guests than those at Morton's and Ruth's Chris. Fleming's in Newport Beach, California, caters to the beautiful people. Cleverly, it offers 100 wines by the glass. Women drink wine and men go where the women are. I have just given three examples of steakhouses with similar menus; their target markets, however, are very different.

A client of ours in Birmingham, Alabama, owns a chain of successful sports cafés. He claims to know very little about the restaurant industry but has great insight into being a guest. He approaches every decision from the guest's perspective. He even prices his beers according to what he would want to pay. He believes he is representative of his guests.

This innate approach works well for some. The sports café owner utilizes little formality in his craft, though his familiarity with his typical guest gives him an understanding of the intended experience. For most of us, a more rigorous approach is required.

5

DIFFERENTIATING CHARACTERISTICS

Being different is not enough;
you must also not be the same.

At this juncture you have assessed your skills and interests, segmented the market from the consumers' point of view, and defined your target market. From here you might be able to buy yourself a job. Without further conceptual work, you will likely arrive at a me-too business, which simply amalgamates features used in other restaurants. This average restaurant will yield returns equal to the cost of capital. The result is really just a job—a job with tough hours and little upside. You need something distinctive, a differentiating characteristic.

A *differentiating characteristic* is required to compel consumers to include a restaurant in their dining routine. Such a characteristic or characteristics must be powerful and bold. Subtlety of distinction does not attract guests. For a restaurant to be successful, customers must covet the differentiating characteristic, though they may not recognize it by that term. I am often surprised to find that prospective restaurateurs think good food and good service are special. They're not—they're just part of the admission price to get into the game. Being good is necessary but insufficient. An undifferentiated restaurant with good food and good service won't earn an economic profit.

Consider how a friend might describe your enterprise. Someone describing The Cheesecake Factory might comment on the great food, great service, or great design. These are all true, which explains why this brand generates above-average sales. But sales are *well* above average. Being better accounts for some incremental sales but not the $11 million of sales per unit per year. The concept is not only better; it is different.

I think these are the differentiating characteristics of The Cheesecake Factory: (1) multioccasion use and (2) the variety of menu items. These two characteristics are powerful in combination. Take a look around The Cheesecake Factory's dining room. You'll see a preprom couple, families with kids, guests having dessert and coffee, and a table of businesspeople having three-course dinners. Further, reviewing the menu is an all-day process; the menu has nearly 350 items. Adding a few menu items is incremental, but the breadth offered by The Cheesecake Factory is significant. First, it eliminates the "veto vote" by offering something for everybody. Second, it introduces complexity into the purchasing, storing, and production systems that are difficult to master. Third, the variety complements the multioccasion use by drawing customers for snacks, desserts, and drinks during nonmeal hours. Interestingly, as suggested above, most customers don't identify the differentiating characteristics, but they do respond to them.

BAD EXAMPLES

I spent many hours listening to the droning of a CEO of a publicly traded bagel restaurant company. He insisted that his "bigger bagel" was a differentiating characteristic. His company served a five-ounce bagel; its closest competitor served a four-ounce bagel. Was that the idea that the late-night meetings generated? Is it possible that these guys didn't laugh themselves sick at the idea of *Seven-Minute Abs?* Maybe being lampooned isn't so hilarious.

If the reaction to the alleged distinctive characteristic is "So what?" or "Who cares?" be assured that though the product may be different, it is still the same. People eat bagels because they are hungry. When they are no longer hungry, the bagel is no longer of use. Hunger is handily defeated by four ounces. A four-ounce bagel and a five-ounce aren't different—they are exactly the same. If the difference is not valuable, it is worthless. Such was the case with this one-ounce increment.

I wasted another few hours of my life trying to dissuade an otherwise successful entrepreneur from his prospective venture. I was convinced he would destroy his wealth in attempting to overtake Starbucks. Supplanting Starbucks is a tough order, requiring a formidable battle plan. His idea was to create a look-alike that offered crepes. Crepes? I explained that Starbucks was not in the coffee business or the food business. Starbucks is a gathering place. It is a place to sit and lounge in the literal tradition of a pub or public house. Paul Westra, a Wall Street restaurant analyst, coined the term *third-place provider* for Starbucks—a gathering place other than work or home. My advice was lost on the entrepreneur, whose most pressing concern was that I would steal his idea. Trust me, I didn't. Crepes? He launched his first unit in the western United States, and recently I understood he intends to close it as quickly as possible. A specific food and beverage offer is not a differentiating characteristic.

BETTER EXAMPLES

Panera Bread has a differentiating characteristic. It is not the onion bread, though the onion bread is awfully good. The key is that Panera bakes fresh bread daily at each location. Further, Panera's differentiating characteristic is a competitive advantage. The process of making high-quality bread daily is too expensive and too complex for most competitors to copy.

Dylan Prime is a Manhattan steakhouse; it is not, however, in the business of selling steaks. Its business is creating a hip, club-like environment for professionals. Dylan's popularity began with a *Time* magazine article stating that Dylan's patrons all looked like Gap models. A Gap-model clientele is different. A Gap-model clientele is valuable. It makes my steak taste better too. Generally, a steakhouse is characterized by dark wood, dim lighting, and fat guys. A nightclub is marked by dark clothes, dim staff, and thin girls. Dylan was not cool to a hipster nor was it a steakhouse to a gangster. But to Dylan's office-professional guests, it was both. The differentiating characteristic was the fusion of two worlds for customers who were just like us.

A few years ago my partner and I were asked to develop a concept for a hotel project in Los Angeles. Regrettably, the hotel never opened, but it was our best work and illustrates the point. We began by assessing the hotel owners. They were young (under 30) and frequented the hot spots from Los Angeles to New York to Paris. After many discussions, we determined that a high-quality, hip hotel was the way to go. This allowed the owners to stick to their demographic, their comfort zone. Unfortunately, Los Angeles hardly needs another hip hotel. We could not be hip like Standard or compete for the model crowd at the Mondrian. The entire ownership group was composed of ex–Wall Streeters. We had to dig deeper. We had to differentiate.

While working on this project, we were reading consumer behavior literature and statistics. We developed our concept differentiation points based on what we learned:

- The fastest-growing travel demographic is a female business traveler. Today, nearly half of all business travelers are women. Therefore, we would develop a hip hotel for women.
- There has been a convergence of work and leisure. Travel today includes both.

EXAMPLE OF DIFFERENTIATION ANALYSIS

The Thesis of the Concept

Project Hotel is designed to accommodate the needs generated by the confluence of business and leisure. Specifically, we will
construct a hotel that is business oriented while providing comforts
in excess of home. Our concept will attract the 24- to 45-year-old
professional traveler, with special, though nonexclusive, orientation toward women. In short, we will be a hip, business-focused,
women-oriented property:

- **Women orientation.** Full-service spa/Complimentary, on-
  site professional makeup artist/Branded personal care items
  (soap, shampoo, conditioner, etc.)/Accompaniment to guest
  room at check-in, late at night, or when requested/Super-
  vised health club/Honor bar to include five styles of pantyhose and a variety of wines by the glass
- **Business focus.** Data port with dedicated T1 communication
  line/Fax/Copier/Printer/Secretarial/Translating services/
  Palm Pilot cradle/Direct telephone line with personal voice
  mail/Cordless telephone with speakerphone and conference
  call capability
- **Hipness.** Plasma TV/CD player and selected CD library
  in room/Selected book library in room/Timeless, inviting
  décor/Lobby and restaurant with a youthful, upscale energy

Description of the Hotel

As the guest enters the lobby, she immediately notices the welcoming, upbeat ambience. The focal point is the living room with
overstuffed couches and chairs. Other guests are relaxing with a
drink and taking advantage of the magazine and novel library.
Games of chess and backgammon are being played on some of

the coffee tables. Hip music fills the air and the near-instant sense experienced by the guest is "Whew. I made it. I am finally here." The airplanes, the airports, the car service; these are all now part of a gladly relinquished memory. Comfort is now the order of the day.

After a quick check-in, a bellhop escorts the guest to the room. This further promotes the feelings of familiarity and relaxation. On entering the room, the sensation is one of invitation. The furnishings are elegant without a hint of pretension. This is a room to live in, not one to live up to. A living room. A living room with a bed. A really nice bed. There is no pressure here but rather an invitation. The cream-colored duvet on the featherbed is inviting. The leather club chair is inviting. The lighting, the temperature, and the music are all inviting. Music. She almost didn't notice. Robert Miles maybe. The room has a CD player with a music library. The shelf above it houses some select novels. No leather-bound copies of *Moby Dick* here. *A Confederacy of Dunces, The Shipping News, All the Pretty Horses*—these are books to enjoy. At first glance, the room is missing a television. Then the bellhop draws the tapestry on the wall to reveal a six-inch-deep plasma TV. The soundless scene on the TV screen is of tropical fish.

When the bellhop leaves, she finally takes off her shoes. That was a long time coming. She makes a survey of the bathroom. The long countertop displays an array of boutique-crafted personal care products in custom containers. Soaps, shampoos, conditioners, and bath oils are available. A bath. Not a bad idea. Just look at that plush, rich purple bathrobe. A quick trip to the refrigerator: here she finds thoughtful refreshments. A bowl of grapes, bottled mineral water, a pitcher of fruit iced tea, and a Cliffbar are among the nonstandard options. In the honor bar, she sees five styles of pantyhose (just in case). Also, a variety of individual serving wines from known vineyards are available. A quick snack and a bath put the guest in position to get busy working or busy playing. She chooses. She's our guest.

Hotel-Positioning Analysis

Americans are working more now than ever. The unemployment rate is near historic lows despite the expansion of people seeking work. Today, 58 percent of women of working age are in the workforce; unemployment is less than 4 percent; and 42.5 percent of couples (both aged 25 to 54) are made up of two full-time workers. In the same age group, nearly 37 percent regularly work more than 40 hours a week. As work has crept into what is traditionally play time, so has the business environment become more flexible. The workplace is marked by accommodation for flextime, part-time, telecommuting, and the like. Technological advance has created a culture where constant connectivity is less an obligation than a simple fact of life.

HIP HOTEL COMPETITION MARKETING ANALYSIS

Herbert Ypma selected 12 U.S. hip, or trendy, hotels in his book published in 2000—*Hip Hotels.* We analyzed the marketing message of 11 of the 12 properties (Chateau Marmont didn't have brochures readily available) selected as hip hotels in an effort to determine the target market of each property. All properties have been labeled *hip* but only the Mondrian, the Marlin, and the Four Seasons allocated over 50 percent of their marketing message— on their Web pages and in brochures—to distinctive characteristics targeting the business traveler, as shown in Figure 5.1.

WOMEN IN THE WORKFORCE: STATISTICS

- Fifty-eight percent of women are now in the workforce.
- Women make up 40 percent of business travelers (up from 1 percent 30 years ago).

FIGURE 5.1 Marketing Analysis

DISTINCTIVE CHARACTERISTICS	MONDRIAN	HOTEL ASTOR	MARLIN	PELICAN	THE TIDES	SOHO GRAND	FOUR SEASONS	MERCER	HOTEL MONACO	THE PHOENIX	HOTEL REX
Business Characteristics:											
Data Port	IR			IR		Y	IR		IR		
Computer	BC, UR	Available	Available				Available				
Modern Hookup	IR		IR					Y			
Multiple Phone Lines	IR	2 Phones	IR	2+ Phones		Y	2+ Phones	3 2-Line Phones	IR		
Portable Telephone	UR	Available						Y			
Cellular Phone	IR						IR				
Conference Phone	IR						IR				
Speaker Phone						Y	IR				
Voice Mail	IR	IR	IR						Y		
Direct Phone #	BC	IR		IR			IR	IR			
Internet Access	UR	IR	IR				24 Hr. Serv.		IR		
Fax	BC	Available	IR	Y			24 Hr. Serv.				
Copy Machine							1 Hour				
Pressing							Y				
Secretarial Services							Y				
Translation Services											
Personal Business Card and Stationery								IR			
Personal Characteristics:											
WebTV			IR						IR		
Video Games									IR		

Feature						
Printer	BC	IR	IR	IR		
CD Player			IR	IR	Available	Available
CD Library						Some Rooms
VCR			IR	IR	Available	Available
Video Library	IR					
Kitchen						
Fireplace						
Safe		IR	IR		IR	IR
Minibar		IR	IR		IR	IR
Double Insulated Walls		IR		Y	IR	Y
24-Hour Room Service	Y			Y	Y	Y
24-Hour Concierge	Y		Y	Y	Y	Y
Gym	24 Hour			Y	Access	Access
Pool	Y	Y		Y	Y	Y
Oversized Bathroom/Tub					Y	
Garden	Y				Y	
Custom Linen		IR				
Whirlpool		IR			Y	
Branded Personal Care			IR			
Same Day Laundry			Y	Overnight		Y
Topless Sunbathing			Y			Y
Multilingual Staff						Y
Babysitting						
Spa				Y / Full Service		Y
Draped Canopy Bed						Y
Aromatherapy						Y
Afternoon Wine Tasting						Y

IR = In Room   BC = Business Center   Nearby
UR = Upon Request   Y = Yes

- Eighty percent of women business travelers put security at the top of their list of important factors in choosing a hotel.
- Women are more likely than men to incorporate leisure into a business trip (not quantified).
  - Favorite leisure activities (shopping 90 percent, visiting historical/tourist sites 70 percent).
- Forty percent of women business travelers are the primary (if not sole) wage earners in the family.
  - Women who travel have real purchasing power.
- Women feel the positive benefits of business travel far outweigh the negative aspects.
  - The number one benefit is networking (54 percent of respondents).
- Women are twice as likely as men to order room service while traveling alone or on business.
  - Fewer than four of ten did so for safety.
  - More than half described room service as a "fun," "indulgent," and "pampering" amenity.
- Nineteen percent of business trips include kids.
  - This is an increase of 63 percent from 1990 to 1994.

WOMEN IN THE WORKFORCE: PERSONAL TOUCHES

The following is a list of personal touches recommended for women guests. Sources are Wyndam Hotels/New York University, Delta Airlines, iTravel.com, and select travel writers:

General:

- Blow dryer
- Iron and ironing board
- Good lighting and big counter in bathroom for makeup application

- Plenty of skirt and padded hangers
- Full-length mirror
- A robe
- Nice stationery
- Voice mail
- Lights in the closet
- Toiletries to include pantyhose and feminine hygiene products 24/7
- Tea in the morning
- Favorable mention given to branded personal care products

Security:

- Secured, brightly lit parking
- Closely monitored lobbies
- Rooms above entry level and near elevators
- Room numbers never said aloud, always written
- Room keys/cards without the room number
- A call to housekeeping instead of using the door hanger to indicate whether you are in
- Hotel business cards (or matchbook) with address to hand to taxi drivers
- Valet parking or accompaniment to parking lot
- Accompaniment to room when late
- Deadbolts and easily operable window and sliding door locks
- In-room timers for TV and lights
- Bellhop or security to check out entire room when accompanied
- Bedside flashlight
- Indoor viewer (peephole)

Relaxation:

- Inflatable bath pillow and bubble bath
- A good book
- Aromatherapy/Scented candles

- A relaxation CD
- Silk eye pillow
- Bath salts
- Spa treatment
- Fitness facilities (should have attendant)
- Jogging partners provided
- Gym
  - Regular guests may like to store a gym bag between visits
- Pool
- Exercise videos and in-room exercise equipment
- Quiet room (double insulated walls)
- Dark fabric to block light from windows or rim of the door

Business (no different from men):

- Big desk with good lighting
- Nearby electrical outlets
- Phone jack for modem connection
- Telephone on desk to eliminate the need to use the one on the nightstand
- Business center with copying and computing services
- 100-watt or 150-watt bulbs

Business—Women Specific:

- Spas are the networking leisure activity of the businesswoman
  - Don't discount if meeting male clients—they make up 40 percent of business these days.
- Quiet library areas off the lobby where women may do business more comfortably than in their rooms or smoky bars
- Should have a Women's Travel Club and roster for women traveling alone where they can put their names on a list. Those on the list will meet and dine together and/or sight-see, shop, and so on—in other words, network.

Children:

- Babysitting services
- Strollers
- Booster seats
- Food options for kids
- Pager rental
- Children's videos
- Video games for older children

Dining:

- Advise the restaurant you are dining alone and would like to try three specialties of the house with a matching glass of wine.
- Preorder breakfast to arrive five minutes after wake-up call.
- Fruit and water in room on check-in

6

UNDERSTANDING THE GUEST'S EXPERIENCE

God is in the details.

I believe that in conceiving a business, nothing should be left to chance. Restaurant investments are inherently risky, and it is our job as businesspeople to engineer out as much risk as possible. Therefore, when launching a concept, consider the evolution of a customer. How will customers first select your business and how and why will customers make it a part of their weekly routine? I have found that writing a typical guest's experience requires an examination of the nuances of the experience. Further, this exercise helps communicate my vision to my partners, investors, and staff.

The following example describes a hypothetical multiuse restaurant called Comfort Café that prepares, packages, and sells home-style meals for both dining in and takeaway. Orders are placed in person, over the telephone, or via an Internet site. Comfort Café provides a complete meal solution for consumers who lack the time, the interest, and/or the ability to cook for themselves. The company is designed with convenience in mind and demands very little from customers in terms of learning. Although the technology platform is robust, consumers can use as little or as much of it as they wish. Let's trace the evolution of a hypothetical customer.

THE COMFORT CAFÉ EXPERIENCE

Julie heard about Comfort Café from one of the moms at her daughter's soccer game. She was interested because her friend said they found a great place that prepares home-style meals and allows the family to eat together with little effort. Julie works, has two active children, and a busy husband. Comfort Café sounded like just what she needed. She was particularly excited about the option of ordering by phone for curbside pickup or delivery. However, before she would buy the family meal, Julie wanted to get a sense of the place first and determine if the product was worthy of her family.

One day at lunchtime, Julie stopped into Comfort Café to see what it was all about. On entering, she found the restaurant familiar. It looked like the kitchen, of a friend of hers, who had just finished remodeling her home. As her eyes scanned the room, she noticed cupboards, a chopping block, lamps (versus glaring overhead lights), country-style wooden tables, and homey chairs. Moving to the order area, Julie noticed the kitchen area was unique for its openness and home design. The kitchen itself, although an open stage, was filled with home-style equipment as opposed to the ugly steel boxes of most restaurant kitchens. Right away, Julie got it. She understood that Comfort Café was designed with the warmth of a home. "Very clever," she thought. Now for the real test: the food.

The aroma of fresh bread and roasted meat enlivened her sense of smell. This was not the soulless fast-food factory she expected. She loved the menu. She thought to herself, "Man, I could eat just about everything here." For lunch, Julie ordered at the counter a hot pot roast sandwich with melted Havarti cheese on grilled sour dough bread and a side of mixed green salad with homemade lemon vinaigrette. Three minutes later, she was enjoying, without a doubt, one of the best sandwiches she had ever had. Julie had never seen a pot roast sandwich before and now wondered why. It was moist and full of flavor. She was impressed and couldn't wait to order dinner.

For dinner, she ordered a quart of split pea soup, slow cooked with a smoked ham hock, and a large build-your-own dinner salad with a side of house dressing. She asked for the exact ingredients in the salad her family loved—cucumbers, peppers, chickpeas, and carrots. For their entrées she couldn't decide between the fried chicken and the meat loaf. It had been ages since her family had either. The fried chicken had been marinated overnight in buttermilk. If Julie got the fried chicken, she would order coleslaw, biscuits, corn on the cob, green beans, and mashed potatoes, just like meals she had had growing up. She knew the mashed potatoes were real because she was watching the cook make them in the open kitchen. The meat loaf had a gorgeous glaze of housemade ketchup. She felt that the meat loaf would be great with the double-stuffed potatoes, corn pudding, and baby peas. Julie decided on the fried chicken for that night and put in her order for the meat loaf to be delivered the next day. This was the most fun she had had planning dinner since the kids were born.

Julie loved the food and was glad to have found a reliable way to outsource the family meal. The entire family was happy to have a low-stress solution for sharing a meal together around the dinner table. Over time, Julie evolved from in-store ordering to ordering by phone for pickup. Later, she placed orders by the telephone for home delivery, the same way she was used to ordering pizza. This process was easy and followed her pace.

Julie found that ordering dinner for pickup or delivery was a true convenience, allowing her to schedule her orders for pickup when she was running errands, for pickup by her husband on his way home from the office, or if they were both too busy to stop by the store, for delivery that evening. Dinner could be arranged anytime from one hour to one week in advance. The family has created a personalized lasagna dinner that accommodates the taste preferences of each family member. Comfort Café remembers the whole lasagna dinner from drinks to entrées to sides and desserts. Yet it's simple for Julie to make a change.

Today, Julie regularly orders dinners for scheduled pickup or delivery. Julie's husband visits Comfort Café regularly for breakfasts, lunches, and coffee. Julie's employer has used Comfort Café extensively for catered events at the office; her coworkers routinely have lunches delivered to their office. Very soon, the convenience, quality, personalization, and affordability of Comfort Café made it Julie's first choice for meal solutions for her family.

7

CRAFTING A CONCEPT

*Much of a restaurant's success is predicated on all
aspects of the concept being in concert.*

This chapter outlines the process
and the many elements of concept development. The information provided is an amalgamation of concepts I have developed,
and, with the exception of Gethin Thomas, the names have been
changed.

In 2000, a restaurant manager called to let me know that the
owner of his restaurant was going to sell the property. He owned
both the real estate and the business. He had been covering losses
generated by the restaurant and decided that he would be content to simply collect rent. Over the next month the owner and I
negotiated the buyout of the business and a new lease. I looked
long and hard at the property to determine the optimal concept
for the location. Here's what I knew:

- The restaurant was designed by a famous Chicago architect.
- It was located one block from one of the largest financial
  services firms in downtown Chicago.
- It was in a warehouse neighborhood with very little residential.

- It was located on the corner of two one-way streets.
- Parking was difficult and taxis were scarce.
- The restaurant had housed two failed concepts—a tony one by a celebrity restaurateur and a local, Nantucket-style fish restaurant.

I needed to create a concept that would include the following:

- Had at least a $50 check average (As a result of the design, I believed that we would be considered expensive regardless of the check average. Therefore, the concept needed to generate revenue commensurate with this perception.)
- Appealed to the 5,000 workers in the proximate investment bank (to secure weekday business)
- Acted as a destination location (to secure weekend business)
- Was easy to execute with the existing management team

The manager was from the prior restaurant. I had no intention of working on the property full-time, so I had to ask the four questions provided in Chapter 2 about the manager—not about me. He came from a restaurant family and had years of experience in trendy Chicago restaurants. Listening to the manager, I became aware that he was a meat-and-potatoes guy. He and his friends preferred to dine at steakhouses and classic Italian restaurants rather than trendy and/or celebrity-chef-driven establishments. He got excited about a great steak, not about foie gras or caviar.

It occurred to me that steak might be my answer. A steak restaurant was high end, appealed to the masses, would require very little capital improvements to the facility, and was a concept that my manager would have credibility operating. Chicago, however, was saturated with steakhouses. Our concept could not survive as just another steakhouse. We had to give it a compelling signature to lure guests away from the competition.

One friend called to suggest I make the restaurant Latin with an entertaining ceviche bar. A colleague suggested an upscale oyster house. The manager suggested we launch a French bistro featuring steak frite. None of these concepts felt right. I believed the Latin restaurant would alienate the investment bank crowd but might generate a destination following. A fish house was the most recent failure at that location. The French bistro could attract the investment bank crowd, but it would never create a destination following. Both groups were critical. Without the investment bank customers, it would be slow on weeknights. Without destination customers, it would be slow on weekends.

As I looked at the restaurant late one night, I was awed by the design. The lighting created shadows throughout the dining room, and the seating was primarily rich red leather banquettes. I began to think about how women would react to this dining room. We were a steakhouse, but we were not a high-testosterone men's club. We were elegant. It came to me that we were a steakhouse for women. That was it. We were downtown, so we had to be hip and target women. In short, we designed a woman-friendly, hip, downtown steakhouse, which we named Kathryne. Next, I had to "peel the onion" to understand what the restaurant's three defining characteristics meant. To do this, I created a Triangle of Definition (see Figure 7.1).

As I looked at the Triangle of Definition, I knew I had to understand the concept in more detail before I could explain it to the operators, marketing team, culinary advisor, and investors, so I developed a Brand Schematic (see Figure 7.2).

Creating the Brand Schematic, although a tedious process, required that I fully developed the brand, the market, and the competition. The Brand Schematic demanded that I wrestle with questions regarding Kathryne's value proposition, its competitive advantage, its day parts (i.e., breakfast, lunch, happy hour, dinner, late night), and the steakhouse market. I was now able to communicate the concept to the department heads and guide the business conceptually. I could also identify concept disconnects quickly.

You don't have to spend as much time as I did putting the information into a brand schematic, or graphic format. A list of the

FIGURE 7.1 Triangle of Definition

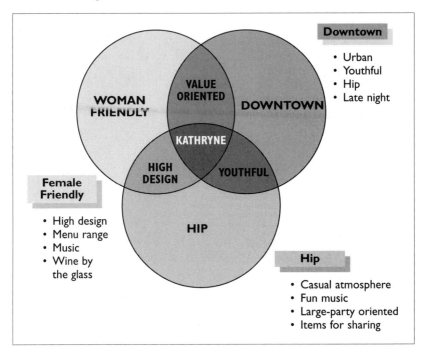

concept's defining characteristics with bullet points further defining each characteristic will complete the exercise perfectly.

In creating the Brand Schematic, I began by listing critical decisions and various elements of the business. For example, in determining our hours of operation, I analyzed four potential day parts. I knew our primary day part would be dinner service. Next, I determined the secondary day parts, analyzing the relevance of each service to the overall business. Which services would both contribute to the strength of the brand and provide incremental revenue? Because Kathryne was designed to be a hip, woman-friendly, downtown steakhouse, I believed that happy hour and late night would be critical to the strength of the brand and provide incremental revenue. Lunch, however, was not a logical day part for the following reasons: (1) A lunch purchase decision is generally a result of convenience and value pricing. Remember,

FIGURE 7.2 Brand Schematic

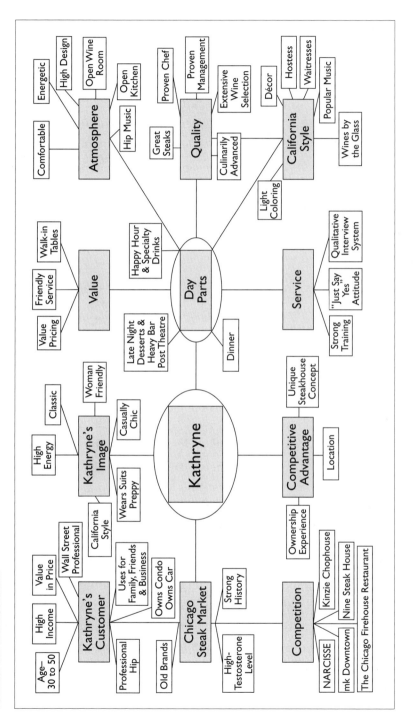

Kathryne was off the beaten path and far from office buildings. There didn't seem to be enough customers working within a five-minute walk or drive from Kathryne. (2) Kathryne tried to attract a youthful, late-night crowd. This crowd is more likely to eat at their desk than eat an expensive steak lunch (like the CEO of their respective companies), and I also considered whether one service would cannibalize another. I needed to determine whether I could attract and retain enough high-quality wait staff to service both lunch and dinner. Would offering a lunch service as a secondary day part dilute the quality of service offered in my primary day part? Further, will guests who spend $14 at lunch spend money at dinner, or will they look for a new dining environment? The exercise of developing a useful brand schematic required that I peel the onion and be as honest and realistic as possible.

CHEFS

I was ready to contact a consulting chef for Kathryne. In the kitchen, I needed a culinary concept, a menu, recipes, food cost worksheets, inventory sheets, and a unit-level chef. I wanted to develop the concept, menu, and recipes before I hired the unit-level chef, because I didn't want this individual to hold me hostage, and I wanted to own the learning. What generally happens is an owner hires a chef. The chef writes the menu with no worksheets (because most chefs are not trained to operate with any corporate responsibilities) and no recipes (because the more information the restaurant has about the recipes, the less valuable the chef is to the restaurant). The owner then invests a significant amount of money in the chef's marketing. The better the owner markets the chef, the more value the chef believes he or she brings to the business. Before you know it, the chef is demanding a raise and/or equity interest in the business as well as explaining to the owner his or her many other career options. If the owner doesn't pay the ransom, then the chef leaves with the staff and takes the recipes.

Further, what I needed was a very targeted menu that was hip, downtown, and woman friendly—not simply what a unit-level chef felt like cooking.

I selected Gethin Thomas to be the consulting chef. He is a highly qualified chef who is not only a good friend (and now my brother-in-law) but has a tremendous business mind for culinary operations. We agreed that the menu needed to be distinctive when compared with other steakhouses and significantly more fun based on our projected youthful clientele and the nightclub music we were going to have. The only other suggestion I had for Gethin was that he create elements of sharing. Shar-

> **Unit-Level Chef versus Corporate-Level Chef**
>
> I define a unit-level chef as the chef who will be in charge of the kitchen but not necessarily in charge of the recipes or concept.
> I define a corporate-level chef as the chef responsible for the menu concept, recipes, and key purveyors but not day-to-day operations.

ing generates interaction at the table and creates a fun style of dining. Two weeks later we had our menu and culinary concept. Gethin developed a menu with four sections (see Figure 7.3): *For the Table, Sample Appetizers, Entrées,* and *Sample Accessories.*

I loved the menu. It was truly a unique steakhouse. It had elements of sharing. It was tailored to women; and the combination of the exotic with comfort food made the menu contemporary and hip. In addition, the menu offered a new twist—the Cappelli (Italian for hat). Gethin developed a number of toppings that could be roasted on a steak like a crust or hat. Now we had our concept. I knew I could promote the restaurant as a hip, downtown, and woman-friendly steakhouse, and I believed the media would love the Cappelli as a menu twist for steaks.

A few weeks later we began to meet with the graphics design firm. The firm would design our menu covers, logo, business cards, and all other forms of corporate communication. I spoke to the designers in great detail about the concept and the customer. I wanted to give them the best opportunity to be successful with

S *e l e c t i n g   a*   **C** *h e f*

In selecting a chef, attempt to determine not only if the chef is creative but if he or she can be creative within the realm of your concept. I often find that the success of the operation is secondary to (1) chefs' creative freedom and (2) the press and publicity they can derive from their creative freedom.

In the event you have concluded that Gethin was our corporate chef as a result of our friendship, I have to state that by the time I developed Kathryne, I was past working with friends. I needed to work with the best, and I determined that Gethin was the best, and our friendship was merely a plus. Gethin's approach to the menu should be noted. Before discussing menu items, Gethin needed to know: Who is the target customer? What is the projected check average? Where is the location? What is the targeted food cost? What is the design concept? What equipment and kitchen facilities did the restaurant have? It was only after he had determined the answers that he began to create the menu. You would be amazed by how many chefs don't consider these questions or, worse, want to discuss their dream concept as opposed to a concept that is in concert with the real estate and the investment.

I prefer that a corporate chef develops the menu rather than a unit-level chef. The corporate chef's incentives are easily aligned with the investor's, whereas the unit-level chef may have motives other than profitability—even if the unit-level chef has an incentive-laden contract.

this project. They, too, exceeded expectations. They developed a black velvet menu cover that had round edges and looked like a jewelry box. It was perfect.

THE KATHRYNE EXPERIENCE

The restaurant opened to great fanfare. Two guests came to Chicago and stayed at a hotel 20 minutes away. After sightseeing

FIGURE 7.3 Kathryne Menu

KATHRYNE

BEGINNINGS

FOR THE TABLE

Appenzeller and Gruyère Cheese Fondue 14

SAMPLE APPETIZERS

Poached Asparagus with Tomato Vinaigrette 8

Bibb Lettuce with Maytag Blue Cheese, Pears
and Spiced Walnuts 8

Tomato and Baby Arugula Salad with Goat Cheese
and Red Wine Vinaigrette 8

Tender Friseé Salad with Bacon, Caramelized Pearl Onions
and Poached Egg 10

Maryland Crab Cake over Pickled Fennel Salad 12

Steak Tartare with Nearly Classical Garnishes 14

KATHRYNE MEATS

ALL OUR BEEF IS DRY AGED AND
CHAR BROILED TO YOUR SPECIFICATION.

• Prime Rib-Eye 12/16 oz. 23/27 •

• Argentinean Filet Mignon 7/11 oz. 24/28 •

• New York Strip 12 oz. 26 •

• Kansas City Strip (Bone In) 18 oz. 28 •

• Colorado Rack of Lamb 28 •

• Veal Chop 24 • Center-Cut Pork Chop 22 •

• Organic Young Chicken 18 •

KATHRYNE SEAFOOD

• Atlantic Salmon 24 • Grade A Tuna 26 •

• Head-on Jumbo Shrimp 27 •

• Whole Cold Water Lobster MP • Market Fish MP •

(continued)

FIGURE 7.3 *Continued*

SAUCES $2

• Red Wine Sauce • Herb Béarnaise •

• Preserved Lemon Hollandaise • Au Poivre Beurre Rouge •

• Black Truffle Sauce • Shallot Bordelaise •

CAPPELLI $3

WE RECOMMEND THE FOLLOWING ACCENTS—IT'S UP TO YOU

Meat
• Maytag blue &
roasted shallots •
• Parmesan, garlic
& basil •

Fish
• Roasted garlic, mint
& lemon •

**For Meat
or Fish**
• Wild mushroom, chervil
& truffle •
• Gremolata •

SAMPLE ACCESSORIES $6

24-hour Tomatoes with Crumbled Maytag Blue

Fricassee of Wild Mushrooms

Creamed Spinach

Spring Peas with Mint and Crème Fraîche

Crispy Fries with Roasted Garlic Aioli

Creamy Yukon Gold Mashed Potatoes

Macaroni and Cheese

all day, they were filled with anticipation—they would be dining in a hip downtown Chicago steakhouse. As a result of Kathryne's overwhelming popularity, their concierge spent hours on the phone securing the guests' reservations.

For the guests, the Kathryne experience begins immediately. The first impression is visual, as they notice a dark candle-filled lounge. Next, the guests hear the upbeat, trendy music. The aroma of roasted meats and the sound of shaken martinis tantalize the guests' senses.

The guests begin their experience at the bar. They gaze at the selection of cocktails. As they watch the bartender prepare orders for the dining room and the bar area, they discuss the many items they have to try tonight. They decide on a Manhattan and an apple martini. They watch as each cocktail is prepared with cheflike precision. They agree that Kathryne's cocktails are the perfect way to begin an evening in Chicago.

Next, our couple moves into the dining area. Their table allows them to voyeuristically participate in the energy of the restaurant. They watch as the bar begins to fill with guests drinking and enjoying appetizers. They turn their attention to the wine room, where the wine steward pulls bottles from a gigantic glass-enclosed display. Our couple elects to try the Kansas City strip—an 18 oz. bone-in steak topped with a blue cheese and roasted shallot cappelli—and a veal chop with a wild mushroom cappelli. The cappelli is the signature topping offered at the restaurant to enhance the taste of a guest's meat or fish. Even though they know that they have ordered too much food for two people, our couple can't resist ordering three side orders—spring peas with mint and crème fraîche, 24-hour tomatoes with crumbled Maytag blue, and creamy Yukon Gold mashed potatoes.

After their meal, the guests are drawn back to the trendy music in Kathryne's lounge. Here they enjoy a late-night cocktail and relax on comfortable couches.

The "Guest Experience" illustrates how the guest will use the restaurant. It highlights the type of service and the amenities that the concept needs to meet its guests' expectations.

When I work with restaurant companies or dine in restaurants, I often find disconnects, meaning that not all aspects of the business are in concert. Here is an example of a disconnect: the location is the Midwest, the décor is conservative, the average guest age is over 50, and the check average is high, yet the menu features the wild, architecturally designed creations of a 24-year-old chef who has an affinity for chilies. Perhaps classic food that is recognizable and conservatively presented is a better fit for the location, décor, and clientele. The only reason for disconnects is the lack of a clearly defined concept. At Kathryne, the design, check average, location, menu, corporate communication, and music are all consistent with the overall concept. In 2001, Kathryne was named Best Steakhouse in Chicago's Citysearch and received such media quotes as "a hip steakhouse catering to fondue eating" and "not your father's meatery."

FORMING THE TEAM

8

WHAT TYPE OF ENTREPRENEUR ARE YOU?

"Who has a partner has a boss."
Proverb

In Part Two, you developed your restaurant as a seamless web, integrating all conceptual elements to deliver a brilliant customer experience. Well done. No matter your level of experience or confidence, you must form a team to realize your dream. The theme of this third part then is self-assessment.

Interestingly, many people believe that management consultants and investment bankers are good businesspeople. Generally, they are not. Consultants and investment bankers are managers. They are most often smart, generally well paid, and in business school learn a trade. They work in teams and make decisions by committee. However, my MBA program, as an example, did not even present, much less teach, the true issues of entrepreneurship. I wasn't told that I would make a lot of money one day and lose it overnight. I wasn't told about the choice between buying chickens for the restaurant and paying the mortgage on my home. I wasn't told to have legal agreements drawn to protect myself from friends. I wasn't told what a truly gut-wrenching, mentally draining process it was to build a business. My teachers taught skills, and we students learned how to analyze problems. Most of us became qualified to be assistant coaches. An entrepreneur, however, is a head coach—*the* head coach.

I meet aspiring entrepreneurs almost every day. Within seconds I can determine which type of entrepreneur each is. Each falls into one of two broad categories: Type 1 or Type 2. Type 1 entrepreneurs insist that a project is about them and that everyone must follow in order to succeed. Type 2 entrepreneurs believe that their team is paramount and compile as many good people as they can find. My bet is always with the Type 1 entrepreneur. As a matter of classification, I call the Type 1 entrepreneur an autocrat and the Type 2 entrepreneur a democrat. (Note that *democrat* is in lower case and bears no relation to the political party in the United States. It simply reflects a philosophy of governance.) If this book is part of your restaurant reading list add *The Prince* by Niccolo Machiavelli and *The Art of War* by Sun Tzu. I believe that these books illustrate strategy in autocracies. And I believe *The Art of War* should be read a second time as a guide to competitive strategy.

The entrepreneurial style is most often revealed by organizational structure. A democrat brings in partners. An autocrat hires employees. A democrat needs partners where he or she lacks skills and wants them for support, to share blame, and to diversify risk. An autocrat believes the greatest risk is in diluting his or her strategy. Whereas the democrat builds a team and then tactics, therefore, an autocrat begins with a strategy and then hires lieutenants to execute it. Autocrats are characterized by profound confidence in themselves and their vision. No good restaurant unit is operated as a democracy. I am only suggesting that an autocracy is the proper approach for a start-up. I am not suggesting that an autocracy is appropriate for an established concern.

Autocratic entrepreneurs have an almost pathological quality. They will risk everything on their ability, and should they lose everything, they will wake up the next morning dreaming of their next project. Similarly, a lawsuit will be of little concern—it is simply a fact of business. They have so much belief in their ability that they often put lives in danger. They'll ask employees to move across the country to be part of the dream with little regard for the risks to an employee. They'll ask family members to lend their retirement savings. They'll ask small purveyors to extend credit and generous terms, not taking into account the materiality to a vendor. The ideal autocratic entrepreneurs have the experience and education that will guide them through the maze of business.

Most people reading this will have an instinctive reaction that democracy is good and autocracy is bad. However, at the start-up phase of a business, autocracy is far more effective. A democracy in this situation is a race to the middle. Decisions taken by consensus are restricted by the most conservative voice and are seldom bold or original but, rather, are dumbed down to what has already been done elsewhere. As the saying goes, "A camel is a racehorse designed by a committee." In any case, those governed by autocracy have explicitly elected it. They voted by writing a check.

I learned about perseverance and the life of the entrepreneur from Chef Douglas Rodriguez. Over many years, I marveled at Douglas's ability to handle the ups and downs of business as if it were a common part of everyone's day. He may have one restaurant with poor sales and another with irate investors. He may have lost a restaurant manager with no notice or had to put in his own money to make payroll. He treats these events as if they were nothing. I would explain such events as one restaurant was failing, we may be getting sued, and we had to make a capital call. Douglas's response to the three problems would be, respectively:

1. "I can fix the problem restaurant."
2. "I'll speak with the investor; she loves me."
3. "This week will be great; we don't need a capital call."

His outlook was driven from prior success and extreme confidence. Frankly, I believe, his confidence may have created difficult situations occasionally. However, his willingness to bet on his many talents is as important as his culinary skill. The combination of these two traits is why Douglas is considered among the world's best chefs.

I got to know Steven Starr of Philadelphia a few years ago. Steven operates a privately held restaurant company that achieves cash flow margins that are among the highest in the business. Steven is profoundly confident and is the sole leader of his organization. He is a perfect example of an autocratic leader. Steven can guide the chef through menu development as well as direct the public relations department. He never second-guesses himself and demands that every aspect of his business be operated flawlessly.

I have spoken with chefs who resent Steven's intrusive style. They find it difficult to be given culinary notes from a culinary novice. Whether Steven understands classic culinary technique is unimportant; he understands his guest. He is a brand manager. He guides his chefs through the eyes of his guest. Steven, as a typical autocrat, doesn't rule with an iron fist. He hires experts for their advice but accepts that the fate of the company rides on his shoulders. In my mind, Steven's willingness to make tough decisions and accept responsibility for all outcomes is the key reason he is one of the top restaurateurs in the country.

Perhaps the best way to assess your entrepreneurial spirit is through your risk tolerance:

- Are you willing to bet everything on your ability?
- If you lose everything, will it affect your outlook in the future?
- If you lose investors' money knowing that you did the best job you could, would you focus on a way to repay the investors or on thinking of your next project?
- If you learn you may be sued, will you lose sleep that evening?

I hope the respective replies of the autocratic and democratic entrepreneurs are apparent. Managerial skills are important in support of the entrepreneur initially and later are critical in building a company from a project. Being a democrat isn't shameful—it is simply not entrepreneurial. Being a democrat doesn't mean you can't run a restaurant company—but you shouldn't at the start-up phase. The risk involved and the emotional toll of these ventures are more than most of the world can imagine. Following a dream can be a lifelong proposition that will most likely end in failure. True entrepreneurs find the thrill in the journey and have the stamina and emotional makeup to treat business ups and downs as if they were on a smooth ride. In short, this life is not for everyone.

9

THE CRITICAL POSITIONS

You need only a few good men.

At the unit level, restaurants have two—and only two—key positions: chef and general manager. Depending on concept characteristics, such as the degree of menu difficulty, the chef may be known as a kitchen manager and the general manager as the unit-level manager. For instance, a unit of the restaurant chain Roy's needs a chef, whereas a unit of the restaurant chain Baja Fresh needs a kitchen manager. Baja Fresh has relatively simple culinary needs and therefore succeeds with a significantly less expensive individual running back-of-the-house operations.

CHEF

Let's begin by reviewing the expectations for a chef in the Roy's model. The chef is the manager of all things related to cooking. The chef should

- know how to operate and, in most instances, provide simple repairs for a kitchen appliance;
- be comfortable ordering, storing, and cooking all ingredients on the menu;
- manage all back-of-the-house staff;
- train all back-of-the-house staff;
- be able to work every station with the limited exception of pastry, where only an understanding is required;
- manage back-of-the-house labor cost to the budget; and
- manage food cost to the budget.

In a restaurant like Roy's, the chef should be a charismatic leader and must be the best cook in the kitchen. The chef should have a passion for food. The chef should walk around the restaurant preservice and share with the entire staff what the perfect scallop or green bean looks like. The chef should receive calls at all hours of the night from purveyors who have just gotten hold of rare or extraordinary items, such as six albino salmon from 15 miles off the coast of Oregon. The chef should have a demanding personality that won't accept even a smudge on the rim of a plate, no matter how busy the restaurant is. The chef's philosophy must be that only perfect product comes from his or her kitchen; otherwise, it goes in the bin.

Today, most chefs come out of culinary academies and want to skip a critical step in their development: mentoring. I wish they would realize that an offer for a chef's position right out of culinary school is not a compliment. What type of restaurant would want a recent culinary graduate heading its kitchen? Certainly not a very good one. It takes years for a cook to become a chef. I don't think most cooks can claim the title before they're 40 years old. In their 20s, a chef-to-be should be traveling and finding as many culinary experiences as possible. In their 30s, they should be learning their trade and settling into a specific style of cooking. In their 40s, they should be good cooks. Cooking is a difficult trade. No two ingredients are ever the same. On Tuesday the sea scallops could be as firm as sirloin, and on Wednesday they could be watery. It takes years for chefs to get a feel for all the ingredients they will be working with. Most likely, if Wednesday's scallops are cooked in precisely the same manner (the same heat and same pan) that cooked Tuesday's scallops to perfection, Wednesday's scallops will steam and be tough. To the bin.

More often than not, I find that restaurateurs hire the most culinarily talented chef regardless of the restaurant's positioning. For instance, I have heard sports bar owners brag that their chef was trained at a prominent culinary school and spent years working for a prominent chef in a fine-dining atmosphere—a recipe for disaster. I guarantee that these sports bars will have high food cost, high labor cost, and high turnover simply because the owners or general managers let their ego do the hiring. Ask yourself what type of highly trained chef would want to cook chicken wings in an undersized (if efficient) kitchen with a staff plucked from Wendy's? The background, abilities, and aspirations of the chef must complement the concept.

Owners often lie to themselves. They believe that their bar will generate a reputation for good food. The food will likely be superior to other sports bars in the area, but nobody cares. Owners never consider the characteristics on which their business competes. In a sports bar, a guest wants cheap beer, a wide selection of ball games, and discounted food. Serving fresh chicken wings (versus frozen) is not a key competitive characteristic nor is the availability of a roasted portabella mushroom sandwich with a basil aioli on a freshly made roll. Any self-respecting chef that accepts a job in a sports bar will quit after a few months but more likely will get fired when the owner learns how much manpower it takes to cook a chicken wing under a highly trained chef.

The right person for that sports bar job is what I call a "hump." A hump is

- a fast cook on the hot-food line;
- willing to do everything and stay as late as necessary;

- generally someone with no formal culinary training;
- someone with many years of cooking experience in similar restaurants.

A hump won't come to the owner to suggest that the menu be rewritten using only fresh, high-quality ingredients.

I made a mistake at Dylan Prime when I hired a chef who saw herself as a presence on the New York culinary scene. Dylan Prime is a steakhouse, not a culinary experience. The food is innovative relative to other steakhouses, but it doesn't attempt to deliver a culinary experience as do New York's Gotham or Gramercy Tavern. Guests go to Dylan Prime for good food and a great experience. During a manager meeting I realized my hiring error. The manager alerted those present that guests in the bar were continually requesting fried calamari. I responded by asking the chef to put fried calamari on the menu and we concluded our meeting. Two weeks later I learned that fried calamari was never added to the bar menu. I asked the chef why she had not added the new menu item, and she told me that she believed it was too pedestrian. I told her to "put fried calamari on the menu" or she was gone.

The next evening I went to the restaurant to taste the new menu item. She had added fried calamari to the menu but had the dish printed as "squid cooked in very hot oil." She believed that wording the dish in a way other than "fried calamari" would protect her culinary reputation. I don't agree at all. Culinary reputations are built on success. Yes, she put fried calamari on the menu, but the guests didn't recognize the dish, and to a person, even after a few drinks, none had a craving for squid cooked in very hot oil. Further, our quickly dismissed chef never considered the difficulty of building a culinary reputation while unemployed.

I am reminded of a story Chef Douglas Rodriquez told me about his first job. Chef Rodriquez began his illustrious cooking career breading chicken at KFC. Not surprisingly, his KFC job didn't last long. Shortly after he began work, he determined that the chicken needed more spices; he went to his mom's spice cabinet to take the "appropriate" seasonings to his work so the Colonel could serve "good" chicken. I believe Chef Rodriguez was terminated (thank goodness) shortly thereafter. Douglas always had higher aspirations and had no business at a KFC. On the other hand, KFC had no business hiring a chef with taste buds.

Remember, a highly trained chef wants to work with good ingredients, be creative, and prepare food that has a high degree of difficulty. A trained chef no more wants to work in a sports bar than Al Pacino wants to do dinner theater in Branson, Missouri. To end where I began—I am shocked how often the mistake of a poor hire for chef is made. The conclusion is not that owners don't know how to hire chefs or that they let their egos get in the way. The correct conclusion is that most owners don't know their guests and what their guests desire from the concept.

GENERAL MANAGER

I view the general manager of a restaurant as the president of a small company. The general manager is responsible for running all aspects of the business. Over the past few years, I've seen the quality of general managers improve. Perhaps our industry and the lifestyle it affords now appeal to types of people who in prior years would have elected a corporate lifestyle. Historically, our industry attracted managers who ended up in restaurants when they ran out of other options. Perhaps they concluded they could better support their drug habit with the consistent pay of a manager than with the ebb and flow of tips as a waiter or bartender. Or maybe a restaurant management job would look great to their parole officer.

Today, managers are recruited from good colleges to run multi-million-dollar businesses. The manager of a Cheesecake Factory could run a business with hundreds of employees, which generates more than $15 million of revenue a year. A restaurant manager at Outback Steakhouse is a partner in the business with a significant base pay. These opportunities have begun to attract more talented people than I have seen previously in the industry.

Think about the skills a general manager must possess. A general manager must understand:

- Budgeting
- Scheduling
- Interviewing
- Hiring
- Bookkeeping
- Timeline management
- Financial reporting
- Points of service
- Analyzing customer feedback
- Marketing
- Training
- Managing food and beverage cost
- Culinary technique
- Floor/service management

Skill in these areas is not cultivated as a journeyman manager. It is acquired through education, years of on-the-job training, and continuing education.

Like a chef, the general manager has to fit the job. Nightclubs often hire general managers from fine-dining restaurants. The premise is that a nightclub is going to win with better service—service more consistent with a fine-dining restaurant. Invariably, service goes out the window the first night the business is overcrowded. Nightclubs pride themselves on allowing celebrities and VIPs to conduct themselves as they please. Many times I have watched a celebrity in a nightclub roll a joint at a table with impunity or a nightclub VIP arrive with 20 guests and a reservation for 6. This behavior would never be tolerated in the fine-dining restaurant world. Managers from the fine-dining world will never understand why the owners or promoters or whoever sets the house rules for nightlife allows such poor behavior.

Again, hiring a general manager who doesn't understand the overall business and its guests' demands is a recipe for disaster and high turnover. In the example above, the two worlds of nightlife and fine dining will never understand one another. The business will operate inefficiently until either the head of nightlife or the general manager leaves. Regardless, the fate of the business has been determined, and all that remains is time before the nightclub is for sale or forced to change its concept.

10

COMPENSATION

Restaurant employees view a partnership as an IOU.

Compensation of key restaurant employees, such as general managers and chefs, should have two components: the base and the bonus. The purpose and structure of the base, or salary, is relatively straightforward. The bonus, however, is difficult to arrange properly. The bonus can be made a function of sales or cash flow and could derive from a formal plan or a partnership share. Naturally, the purpose of the bonus is to align the incentives of key employees with those of the business. Often, the opposite is the case.

WHAT NOT TO DO

A number of years ago I was offered a financial package to build a restaurant/lounge. I was to be the last management person hired and was supposed to run all aspects of operations. The president of the company, who made the offer, had recently read a *Crain's New York Business* article stating that the average restaurant manager in New York City earned $38,000 per year. On the basis of this benchmark, he determined that $40,000 per year was a good base pay offer. The bonus award was 10 percent ownership of the restaurant/lounge after the investors were repaid with interest. Remember, I lived in New York City, and New York City is one of the most expensive cities in the world. Also, I had just left Salomon Brothers, a "white shoe" investment bank, to open my own advisory firm. My base salary expectations, not to mention requirements, were far above his offer.

So what about the bonus? On the one hand, 10 percent of the business without capital investment seems lucrative. In this case, however, the offer was simply asinine. First, the bonus was deferred until all the investors were paid. Second, no one except me, at any level of the organization, had ever been involved with a successful restaurant. Third, the management team had already been hired without regard to merit. Investors filled several positions. As I discuss shortly, having key employees invest capital is a clever way to enhance the likelihood of success. On the other hand, hiring an investor because of his investment is a gross misjudgment that will *increase* the likelihood of failure. Money is fungible, so those who provide it are equal. Skills are specialized and must be the factor used to make an employment-partnership offer.

The offer was $40,000 base pay plus 10 percent of a restaurant that would be operated by an inexperienced and unqualified team. In addition, no mechanism existed to turn my 10 percent ownership into cash. I already had a job. I worked for money—that is, my goal was not to accumulate minority interests in restaurant properties. The only plausible buyer of my equity would be one of the remaining partners. The project's success, however, was overwhelmingly dependent on me. My partners would be best served by keeping me involved; in other words, preventing me from taking my "success fee."

In any case, the value of a single restaurant is often its cash flow, because rarely is a single unit sold for a multiple of cash flow.

Typically, a single unit's sale price is the value of the lease. I placed no value on the cash flow beyond my base pay. My exit therefore, if possible, would not be sufficiently lucrative. I figured that $40,000 was one-third to one-half of what it cost me to live in Manhattan, and the bonus didn't offer credible upside.

The moral of this story is twofold: (1) The offer was ridiculous, and (2) had I accepted the offer, I would have quit within months because my household would have been running at a loss. It would have been a disaster for the company to lose its general manager within two months. The only logical alternative for me would have been to treat the job as part-time, collecting my salary while pursuing other projects. Ethically, this route was inappropriate, so I declined the offer. I wondered why the president would put the company in such a compromising position. My guess is that while attempting to generate shareholder value, he unwittingly created risk.

DETERMINING THE BONUS PACKAGE

A few years ago, I had dinner with one of the great CEOs in our industry, Chris Sullivan. I asked Chris what the greatest decision he made at Outback Steakhouse was. He replied that "every night the owners lock the doors at my restaurant." Outback set the standard for unit-level compensation. All general managers at Outback are required to invest cash in their unit. Their investment gives each general manager (GM) rights to a percentage of cash flow (the bonus) that aligns the general manager's incentives with corporate's interests. The bonus portion of overall compensation is substantial enough to keep the GM interested and credible enough to keep the GM motivated.

I suggest that when you think about a compensation package for a potential employee, you consider that, according to hiring experts, happy employees state four reasons for their happiness:

1. "My manager cares about me."
2. "I have a friend at work."
3. "I am in a position where I am good at what I do."
4. "I am recognized for my accomplishments."

I believe that in structuring compensation, personal as well as professional needs must be met. In an interview, I always ask what the person's professional goals are. Invariably, candidates reply that they are going to be the best there ever was, will take the company public, or in some shape or form will take over the world. Next, I ask about candidates' personal goals. The same people who just sounded like the reincarnation of Napoleon say they want to spend more time with their family. Taking a company public and having more family time are inconsistent. In fact, the answers are polar opposites. My experience has been that personal goals always supersede professional goals.

Having discussed goals, I can now begin to craft a compensation package. I consider the following four points:

1. I want employees to work at my business and pay their bills—it shouldn't cost someone money to take a job. I need to be certain that an employee's basic needs are met. That stated, I know from experience that some people simply cannot manage their personal affairs. I believe these people will be similarly incapable of managing their professional life. They are not considered for hire.
2. I want all of our incentives to be aligned. When the shareholders make money, employees should benefit.
3. I want employees to be judged and therefore compensated for what they can control. Specifically, a chef who is compensated with a percentage of cash flow may find it difficult to receive a bonus even if his or her food cost and kitchen labor cost are excellent.
4. I want employees to view the bonus plan as an opportunity to increase their salary substantially. If employees don't

consider the bonus plan credible, then they probably don't believe in my vision and shouldn't be considered for hire.

THE COMPENSATION PACKAGE MAY NOT MATTER

How critical to the success of the organization is the potential hire? If the company is built around the reputation of an individual, then that individual must be made a partner. If the position can be refilled without affecting the business, then an employee is preferable to a partner.

I am amazed by how often I see a restaurant planned by a financial partner, perhaps someone from Wall Street or a real estate developer, who takes the role of president. In assembling the team, this partner negotiates an agreement with a celebrity chef. (Financial partners feel that because the capital is theirs, they should own the entire business.) The reality is that the restaurant belongs to the celebrity chef no matter how the deal is struck. The public will dine in the restaurant because of the chef, and thus revenue derives from the chef. Once the chef's name is involved, the financial partner will no longer have a vote. Therefore, it is critical that the financial partner understand his or her role. In this instance, the compensation package is not as important as having roles, responsibilities, decision making, financial hurdles, and measurement outlined in the operating agreement. Remember, the chef will always have the power unless the financial partner is willing to retool the concept with a new chef. The negative publicity associated with a changing of the guard can be material and the cause of a quick demise in the business.

In determining compensation, Paul Westra influenced my opinion greatly. He and I were negotiating with a talented chef for a restaurant project. I had budgeted $57,000 for the chef's base pay. The chef had asked for $62,000. I don't remember why, but that $5,000 difference was very important to me at the time. I was stuck

on the fact that I really wanted to work with this chef, but I felt
the job should pay less than $60,000. When I told Paul about my
dilemma, he asked what was wrong with me and why I was "nickel
and diming" people. Then he strongly suggested that we make a
$5,000 deposit in the chef's "favor bank." He was right. Such gen-
erosity generates loyalty, which can easily pay for itself quickly. This
story would be better had the restaurant opened and the chef
worked loyally for years. He was pleased that we met his asking
price, but for myriad reasons the concept was never funded.

DON'T GO CHEAPLY

The chef and the general manager are the two most important employees in a restaurant. In my example earlier in this sec-
tion, I related how a restaurant investor looked at the average pay
for a restaurant general manager in *Crain's* business magazine.
Why would anyone want to hire an average person for a critical
position? It is an average person, after all, who works for an average wage. No one is proud of a new Ford Taurus or a recent stay
at the Holiday Inn. Similarly, no one is proud of an average wage
and will produce accordingly. What better way to deliver a me-too
project that earns zero economic returns? I want to hire someone
who values his or her skills and time, not someone who will work
for an average wage. Further, in contrast to a favor bank, a mod-
estly paid chef or general manager may well create a "grudge
bank" and problems far beyond a few thousand dollars a year.

11

DON'T BE A GUINEA PIG

Hold employees to their sales pitches.

Potential key hires, the chef and the general manager, will try to dazzle you and convince you that they will drive revenue, cut costs, and work untold hours. If candidates have previously accomplished what they claim they will, there is a chance for a repeat performance. But if no historic evidence of success exists, be wary. As a friend's college recruiter insisted, "Performance predicts performance." In other words, the best proxy for future success is past success. Investigate three things about a prospective employee: track record, track record, and track record.

I have become extremely jaded about hiring. Most of the world wants to be recognized today for a job they will do tomorrow. Why is that? Chef Bob Kinkead always told his cooks that the title Sous Chef would be conferred after one of them had been doing the job of sous chef for a year. He meant that if you took the responsibility and claimed the position, he would acknowledge it. This approach works exponentially better than awarding a position to somebody with the expectation that he or she later earns it. Chef

Kinkead's approach is optimal where the staff has been assembled and working together for some time. In start-up ventures, generally, you will be only vaguely acquainted with the majority of your staff. This lack of personal knowledge means that interviews, references, and résumés are your best means of predicting a candidate's success in your organization. Unfortunately, most potential hires would have you believe there is no relationship between past failure and future (expected) success.

If you are planning a business in the world's most competitive industry, consider that the odds say you will lose a great deal of money and close the restaurant within a few years. You are Rocky Balboa versus Apollo Creed. You have competitors that are better financed, have long-established reputations, and own better locations. You have no margin for error. Remember, Rocky lost the first fight. Therefore, you can't make a mistake in hiring—particularly for key positions. You have to find great people with proven track records. Be suspicious about potential hires who understand what the interviewer wants to hear. Don't believe their claims of a lifelong dream of success for your company.

I become aggravated listening to what potential hires can do for me. I quickly correct them and let them know they can't do *anything* for me. Rather, I can give them an opportunity to help themselves. Over the years, I have made plenty of mistakes. I have listened to salespeople articulate the top-line benefit of their skills. Too often I bought the pitch. It took years for me to realize that if these people could really do what they said, they would have done it before (are they pacing themselves in their career?) or they wouldn't need me, because they could lead an organization on their own. I have hired self-proclaimed "great" managers who couldn't keep a staff. I have hired bartenders who claimed they had "a huge following" that would generate huge sales. One was so persuasive that I nearly allowed myself to dream of early retirement but discovered he was simply a drunk. The true stars of this industry have to never sell their value. They have done it before, and the expectation is that they will do it again. Don't be a guinea pig.

If your candidates had the abilities they proclaimed, they would have succeeded before—track record, track record, track record.

My father always said that success is transferable. The trick is learning the art of success. As I stated previously, this industry is filled with life's unfortunates. However, this need not be the case. I have had tremendous success hiring people who have had success in other industries. For instance, I hired a talented baker who was previously a pharmacist and an effective marketing director who had been a technology entrepreneur. Perhaps the most creative partner I have had in this industry was a CPA, of all things. All of these people knew what it took to be successful and applied their ability to the restaurant industry.

EXPECT NOTHING

Begin your interviews with the belief that candidates are full of baloney. Ask a few questions and listen to them talk. Ask where they did what they claim as accomplishments. They are most likely exaggerating their potential. Generally, credible people speak in detail, whereas people who are exaggerating (or lying) speak in the abstract. Listen and determine whether potential hires are selling their plan for success in your company from altitude or from the ground. When management candidates highlight the importance of a training program, ask how they would develop that program. The correct answer will address daily routines rather than a one time preopening event.

Training must include a calendar or some sort of timeline. The manager should know that the staff must master guest interaction before points of service. The manager should discuss daily testing and ways to measure the success of the training program. The theme of the correct answer is that training must be institutionalized, not simply left up to the charisma or whim of the manager. The wrong answer will be a broad statement on setting a high standard and trailing the staff very closely.

Chefs are notoriously full of themselves—full of baloney. They will say that their food was the reason that their last restaurant was successful. I had a chef candidate tell me that he was the force behind one of the Olives restaurants. I suppose I was to believe that the restaurant's success had nothing to do with the company's marketing machine or the fact that Todd English is a poster boy for the industry. A good chef understands the correlation between marketing and food. In most restaurants, the menu alone is intended to drive sales.

Listen to your chef candidates discuss their relationships in the industry. They should mention their access to staff, product, purveyors, and the media. Certainly, they need to be good cooks and understand costs, but that bit is easy compared with marketing the product.

12

A DEAL MUST BE MATERIAL TO AT LEAST ONE PERSON

Be careful what you wish for.

A recipe for disaster: a group of successful people getting together to open a restaurant. The plan is that the team comprises individuals with demonstrated success in all functional disciplines needed for the enterprise. Each person keeps his job but devotes a limited amount of time to the business, thereby reducing personal financial risk. The time investment, though limited, is expected to suffice, saving the business the cost of several salaries. I frequently see this pattern arranged by Wall Street employees, but the plan never succeeds. Once the going gets tough, the deal isn't big enough for any one person to care. Remember that each partner retains a high-paying position elsewhere. This restaurant hobby is as easily discarded as a used softball mitt. Further, multiple partners add useless layers of bureaucracy to the organization.

Soon after I left Salomon Brothers to form my own restaurant advisory company, I was asked to join a team opening a restaurant in the Lower East Side of New York City. At this point in my career, I had little experience in small business development. As the businessman, I was invited to join an already large cadre of general partners: the chef, the architect, the developer/marketing person, the developer's girlfriend/marketing person, and the manager. I was the last person in, so the deal was "take it or leave it." The chef and the architect were highly accomplished, and I liked the location. Further, we had perhaps the lowest rent per square foot in Manhattan. I took it. I took it eagerly. According to the plan, the celebrity chef would craft a menu and assemble a staff, the architect would build the restaurant, the developer had already negotiated a great real estate deal, and I would conduct business matters.

On paper the deal was foolproof. I will never forget telling my wife, as we looked at the dilapidated building, that this was our nest egg and the opportunity was essentially "free money." I continued to explain that we had a great chef, a great architect, a great location, a great lease deal, and a strong core team. We agreed that very little could go wrong. I came to learn that the influence of fools is seldom revealed on paper.

We took possession of the site in May and intended to open in September. By October we were still not open and were out of money. The entire fourth quarter of that year was spent conducting capital calls. I was issuing new shares, revaluing existing shares, meeting with banks, and placating investors I had never met. In short, I was scrambling, trying to get the restaurant open late and over budget. To make matters worse, I had sold some friends on the deal. You never want to lose an investor's capital, but losing a friend's money is far more painful.

We continued to scramble for money until we finally opened on January 4. We were three months behind schedule ($500,000 in lost sales according to budget), and we had more than $300,000 of trade payables. We had no money for launch events, no money for marketing, and no money to conduct a proper training program. By opening day, the writing was on the wall: We were doomed. To make matters worse, the developer moved to another state. (She certainly had the right to move but may have stayed if the project had been more than a sidelight.) The investment group suffered from a free-rider problem, whereby each individual hoped to be saved by the work of another. Among other things, with the developer's move, we lost our marketing arm. Next, our high-profile chef determined that association with a failed restaurant would be disastrous for his career. He decided it would be best to part before one of the New York papers unfairly painted him as the captain of the Titanic. I don't think this decision was difficult. The failing restaurant couldn't pay him, but his "real" job paid him six figures many times over. Further, he had a book deal that would soon require all of his available time and attention.

To recap, the restaurant owed more than $300,000, lost its marketing arm, lost its celebrity chef, and had a host of disgruntled investors. I was left with the architect, whose job was complete, and one journeyman bartender-turned-manager. Though for me this project was supposed to be one of many, I began to spend most of my time there. I rewrote the brunch menu and worked the brunch shift for many weeks. I asked a senior member of my advisory company to help with marketing ideas, further diluting the capabilities of my regular job. I was throwing everything I had at the project in trying not to lose my friends' money.

I regularly received calls from angry investors with concerns ranging from the temperature of their recent meal to the value of their stock. The vast majority of capital was raised prior to my engagement. Unfortunately, the facts didn't stop irate phone calls from investors I had never met, heard of, or asked for money. Distressed capital erased history and now they claimed they had invested in this business/disaster because of me and expected me to make it right. Placating angry partners whose ammunition is finger pointing and distorted facts is stressful and time consuming.

To end a long story, I lost my friends' money and am no longer a partner. The restaurant is still operating under a different capital structure. Trying to rescue the deal alone cost me hundreds of thousands of dollars in lost opportunities. As you have determined, the moral of this story is not that hard work and a relentless pursuit of success can make your dreams come true. The moral is simply that this deal was not worth enough to any partner for him or her to make the sacrifices that are required to be successful in business. The deal was constructed to be part-time work for a lot of partners. Half of a commitment does not create wealth. Each deal needs one clear autocratic leader. Partners are not necessary other than to align all parties' incentives. In almost every instance, a restaurant deal should have a financial partner(s) and an operating partner. The operating partner may be a chef or a general manager but no one else.

Part Three

LOCATION, LOCATION, LOCATION

13

LOCATION ANALYSIS

A great location is good insurance.

The real estate strategy must be consistent with the concept. Real estate selection is a highly quantitative process that extends far beyond rent per square foot. It requires an in-depth understanding of the concept's target market, traffic patterns, and demographics.

After developing the concept, you must determine the proper location for your business to flourish. The proper location will be in concert with the menu, design, guest throughput, check average, and table turnover rate. First, separate your business by sector—for example, fast food, family/casual dining, or premium dining. A competitive analysis of check average can assist in site selection, but it can't define it. For instance, in the premium sector, Morton's has a real estate strategy different from that of the Chart House. These restaurants have similar check averages but substantially different real estate strategies.

Morton's concept, as previously noted in Chapter 4, is a men's club. It is exclusive and private. Morton's rarely has windows and often selects "B" real estate. When guests approach a Morton's, they notice a small sign and a single heavy wooden door. Before entering a Morton's, they understand the price points, the menu offering, and the experience that awaits. Guests would be confused if they sat down and opened the menu to a selection of sandwiches or encountered kids in the dining room. The intention is to make guests feel like captains of industry. Morton's real estate strategy is effective and consistent with its image—a high-end men's club.

The Chart House is a high-end restaurant that wants guests to have a resort experience. Its locations are, with few exceptions, destinations. The intention is to create a vacation feeling. Guests generally drive great distances but on arrival, whether a mountain location overlooking Denver or a San Francisco location overlooking the Pacific, they'll relax and enjoy the tranquility and elegance not easily attained in a city.

Morton's and the Chart House compete for guests, but each concept's location defines the guests' experience and establishes the guests' expectations.

When considering the proper location for your concept, determine what brands in other businesses are similar to yours. Will your concept be the Wal-Mart of the restaurant world or Tiffany's? Will your concept be The Gap or Kenneth Cole? Brands like Wal-Mart, Tiffany, The Gap and Kenneth Cole have spent millions of dollars determining where to place their stores. I believe successful businesses, with few exceptions, locate where the eyes are rather than trying to attract them elsewhere. Consumers have preferences in sourcing products and services; why try to retrain their behavior? In short, use other brands for guidance; if you have a common customer, study their real estate strategy.

Your location should be convenient to your target market. Most restaurants cater to guests who live or work within five to ten minutes of the property. Locating near your guests is generally optimal. If your concept is designed to cater to middle-income families, locate in communities with the greatest concentration of minivans. Don't make your guests work to dine at your establishment.

When we were developing the Dylan Prime concept, some suggested that we should be a good standard steakhouse. The belief was that if we offered good food and good service, the guest would find the restaurant. An analysis of the location offered different guidance. The location was in a loft area that had only one-way streets. A wrong turn and it could take a while to get back on track. Further, there were very few businesses near the restaurant. Most likely, our guests would have to travel by taxi for ten or more minutes. I wondered what type of guest would work to find a restaurant in a hip area with lofts. I believed the answer was the young executive. Therefore, we needed to develop a concept that appealed to the young executive. A standard steakhouse is appropriate for a more standard location.

In conclusion, when you fully understand your concept, the right location will be apparent. A deal has a limited shelf life, meaning that your investors, employees, and you will become tired of chasing a dream. Most likely, you will need to determine which location other than the ideal location will give your concept the best chance of success. The ideal location is often not available, but that should not be an excuse for not doing your deal. No aspect of your deal will ever be optimal. In real estate selection, we are required to select from available sites, not necessarily our ideal site.

14

"MY LANDLORD SEEMS TO LIKE ME"

"Ask not what you can do for your landlord . . ."

Once the appropriate type of location is determined and a short list of available sites that might work for your concept is drawn, the entrepreneur will negotiate with various landlords to reach a deal. Lease negotiations can be extremely complex. Most often, though, points of contention come down to five terms: rent per square foot, lease duration, landlord contribution, rent abatement, and guarantee.

My objective here is not to offer advice on the particulars of each of these elements but rather to warn about a qualitative factor of negotiations: the personal relationship. Entrepreneurs often believe that fair terms are more likely if a landlord likes them. Not surprisingly, the landlord is most often pleasant and reasonable. Be advised, though, that what *you* might view as an advantageous personal relationship, the landlord employs as a sales technique.

Let's begin by understanding that the landlord is one of a restaurant entrepreneur's primary opponents. A landlord is in the business of collecting rent. His or her concerns are that (1) a tenant will not be capable of paying rent; (2) the tenant's business will dilute the image of the property; (3) the tenant will damage the property during operations; (4) a fixed-rent contract will be less remunerative than a percentage-rent contract; and (5) the tenant will run out of money during the buildout and thus leave less valuable property. The landlord's objective therefore is to attract tenants who have strong operating histories, strong balance sheets, and strong top lines. The landlord will want to know that the tenant can weather a challenging business cycle and any other whims of the economy. In short, a landlord wants The Cheesecake Factory or P.F. Chang's.

If you are an independent operator and aren't being pursued by a facility such as the AOL Time Warner building or the Bellagio Hotel and Casino, you are almost certain to be last on the landlord's wish list. Simply, five-star properties recruit from a short list of five-star restaurateurs. Independent operators, such as Richard Melman of Lettuce Entertain You and Steven Starr (identified in Chapter 8), can provide a landlord with financial comfort. However, these individuals are aberrations in a sea of independents viewed as deadbeats. Most often, an individual or partnership will be relegated to competing for B-type real estate. Even a high net worth individual probably isn't willing to make a personal guarantee for the life of the lease. Such guarantees are often astronomical, but a publicly traded company provides value to a landlord in the form of a corporate guarantee.

Chef Douglas Rodriguez, our partner Tom Nally, and I were negotiating a lease for the corner of 57th Street and 6th Avenue in Manhattan. Sbarro had recently vacated what we thought was a great site. The space was approximately 9,000 square feet and had tremendous foot and automobile traffic. The terms, as originally presented, were onerous, but because the landlord seemed to immediately like Nally, we expected to reach a favorable accommodation. The landlord asked $900,000 rent per year plus 10 percent of sales above $7 million. Further, the landlord wanted a ten-year lease guarantee. Restaurant economics suggest that rent should be in the range of 7 percent of total sales. For all intents and purposes, the proposed rent was not feasible at any reasonable amount of revenue. At $10 million of revenue, the base rent plus percentage rent would be 11 percent; and at $15 million of revenue, the base rent plus percentage rent would have been 10 percent. For those who are mathematically challenged, the guarantee would have resulted in a $9 million liability on execution of the lease. In this negotiation, we faced a sales hurdle well above our expectations with a potential liability that dwarfed any realistic financial gain. For those who are logically challenged, the appropriate response was to pass on the deal. My partners and I walked away.

This result surprised us. Until the very end, we believed we could agree on more favorable terms. Even though the landlord and Nally seemed to have developed a quick friendship, our instincts were, if not wrong, at least irrelevant. The landlord insisted that the terms were not negotiable. He had no incentive to negotiate because he had Sbarro on the hook for the life of the lease—an ideal situation for a landlord. From the landlord's perspective, the friendship served to persuade us, not accommodate us.

Two years ago, I passed on a deal in Las Vegas. A megaresort was in early development off the strip. The development company claimed to have built successful properties around the world. The property in Las Vegas featured beautiful models and was supported by a movie that simulated the feel of the resort at peak occupancy. I was truly amazed. The development company delivered the best dog and pony show I had ever seen, speaking at length about its culture. It was a culture of caring about the lessee, who would be part of a greater family—the lessor's family. Although the renderings were beautiful, I was hesitant. I sought a good property but already had all the family I wanted. I sensed something was amiss with the cultlike belonging the company was so keen to engender. Instead of new buddies, I needed to manage the risk associated with signing on at such an early stage. Remember that the property consisted of models. No tenants had signed, and construction was closer to the beginning than to the end.

I asked how much money the company would give me to open the property. Would it build out the unit? What would it pay for considering the risk was so great? It was willing to provide "very little" besides a few rent-free months. I next asked what happened if the project was not fully leased when the resort opened and the occupancy rate had an effect on traffic? The company people offered to discuss this if and when that got to be the case; that is, after we signed the lease. They continued to state that they wanted me to succeed. They insisted that helping me succeed was their only motivation. I asked for a clause tying my rent to the completion of the project and the occupancy rate. They said no. I asked for names of tenants who had been successful in their resorts and the sales per square foot of these properties. They said there were no good comparisons, so they couldn't give me that information. I passed on the deal.

A few months ago, I took my wife and kids to look at the property. I had only seen it in the planning stages. Friday night about 7 PM, and the resort was empty. Spooky empty as if it were suddenly abandoned. It had not been abandoned though; it simply had never been occupied. Occasionally, we saw a couple walk by, and it appeared that a few people were staying in the hotel, but the resort was practically empty. I was angry as I walked by the failed retail stores and restaurants. I looked at the property as a soldier looks at Arlington Cemetery. I wondered how many people's lives had been ruined by the sales pitch. How many families had their lives changed because of one bad decision? The takeaway? Your landlord doesn't like you. Your landlord needs to lease his space. Your landlord wants his money, and most landlords will go to any length to get it.

Four years ago I signed a lease in Manhattan—priced under market, great location, great traffic. The landlords were an elderly couple who had operated a restaurant and bar at the site for many years. They had neglected the property to the point that it became the dirtiest restaurant I had ever seen. The windows were so greasy as to be opaque. The basement was covered with one foot of standing water. The stench was horrific. New York University students would pack the place every Friday and Saturday night. The bar was a kid's hangout with the reputation of facilitating underage drinking. You'd have to be both young and drunk to tolerate the surroundings for any period of time. The owners seemed very pleased with their business and were hoping that we would operate essentially the same business for many years.

I was horrified that the landlords weren't embarrassed. On a sales-per-square-foot basis, this dump had to be among the worst in the city. Still, the owners had fancied themselves restaurateurs. Each prelease signing meeting took five times as long as it should have. The landlords were retired and liked to combine a lease discussion with the opportunity to show me restaurants they liked. This was interesting. The operators of the most repugnant facility believed that their insights into food (and in particular, for some odd reason, dip) were material to our future business. I suppose a warning light should have gone on—these people didn't see themselves the way the world saw them.

Our plan was to gut the space, bring in high-quality food, and provide a fun and hip experience. We executed the lease and began our design. We had partnered with a highly regarded and nationally known architect whose ideas were spectacular. We were certain that the restaurant would be on the cover of *Interior Design* magazine. The designer had his expeditors file the plans, and we believed we were on our way. Unexpectedly, the landlords' attorney alerted us that the landlords intended to exercise a lease clause requiring landlord approval of all architectural and design plans. I never expected this clause to be an issue. Honestly, how could slumlords object to the plans of one of the country's top designers?

Shockingly, the landlords felt our plans were not detailed enough, although the designs met all the requirements of the city. I went ballistic. Renderings and designs are expensive. In addition, our few months of free rent were wasted trying to get design approval. We were unable to meet our timelines. Fixed expenses were piling up, including interest expense on investor capital. We opened four months late and lost the holiday season. Why did the land-lords cripple our ability to succeed? I still don't know. Maybe they wanted to be respected as restaurateurs or fawned over as real estate barons. Maybe they were just bored old folks who wanted to fill their days. The takeaway? Your landlord has his own agenda. He doesn't like you.

My suggestion is to not fall in love with a space and not be swayed by ephemeral friendship. As in most negotiations, he who cares least wins. Never buy a landlord's story. Sell yours. Let land-lords make a bad deal. Let them overpay and realize that they won't get their percentage rent. Recognize that landlords will tell you any-thing to persuade you to sign the lease. The people who sit across from you, appearing bright and engaging, are your adversaries. I believe the best approach to take with a landlord is one you may take with an investor: a formal presentation. Most landlords I have met are ego driven. They can be persuaded to make a bad lease decision with a proper presentation. Why take my restaurant with no guarantee and pass on a large company's restaurant—ego? A landlord may believe that the tenants in his or her facility are a reflection on him or her. A well-educated and sophisticated land-lord, particularly in cities like New York and San Francisco, may elect to take an independent concept and the prestige that the con-cept brings over a long-term guarantee.

C *h a p t e r*

15

TENANT IMPROVEMENT DOLLARS

Your homework is worth a great deal of money.

An entrepreneur should investigate many avenues of finance. The proposed project is often initially underfunded. Businesspeople routinely pressure trade creditors for extended terms to improve cash flow in difficult times. Prior to operations, your landlord is the best source of noninvestment dollars. Generally, a landlord has money available for the buildout. This money is referred to as tenant improvement (TI), or landlord contribution. TI helps the landlord lease space, but it comes at a cost. The landlord will try to recoup the investment with higher rent and percentage rent. From a net present value perspective, it is almost always better to maximize up-front tenant improvement dollars and pay over time. The reason is that a landlord's hurdle rate of investment is almost invariably less than your investors' hurdle rate of investment. (See sidebar in Chapter 22 for definition of *hurdle rate.*)

Though landlords may claim otherwise, they have money. Trust me, if Chef Jean-Georges Vongerichten wants the space, the landlord will find the money. The question is how much risk the landlord is willing to take. How much TI can you expect? Your analysis should begin with your financial model and then consider the landlord's economic model.

Your financial model depends on the return expected by your investors, including yourself. Anticipate that your buildout will cost between $200 and $400 per square foot, depending on your concept and the condition of the facility. Determine the cost of opening your restaurant in the space under consideration. Let's say that your concept is a 6,000-square-foot, upper-end casual-dining restaurant. For the purposes of example, assume the buildout will cost $250 per square foot ($1.5 million) and you expect to generate sales of $500 per square foot ($3 million). Let's estimate a 12 percent cash flow margin, or $360,000 per year ($3 million sales times 12 percent cash flow margin). This part is easy. You've computed these figures countless times prior to pursuing your entrepreneurial dream. Too often, however, substantially less sophistication is brought to bear in calculating financial returns.

Let's estimate that your investors expect a 25 percent return on investment, and you're giving them 75 percent ownership of the project, retaining 25 percent for yourself. Based on the estimates of cash flow, the investors are entitled to $270,000 annually ($360,000 cash flow times 75 percent ownership percentage). In order to receive a minimum of 25 percent return on invested capital, the investment cannot exceed $1.08 million ($270,000 divided by 25 percent).

So what has been learned? We estimated that opening the restaurant requires a $1.5 million investment, but your investors can't invest more than $1.08 million. Must the dream die? Not necessarily. You need the landlord to contribute $420,000 ($70 per square foot). The landlord may add a few dollars to your rent per square foot, but this trade is generally to your advantage.

An alternative is to increase the investors' ownership percentage. The entrepreneur is, of course, reluctant to do this, as doing so reduces his or her share. In any case, the problem in this instance cannot be solved this way alone. To return 25 percent, an investment of $1.5 million must produce cash flow of $375,000 ($1.5 million divided by 25 percent). This project is expected to generate only $360,000 in cash flow. Best to target TI.

Having analyzed the capabilities of your financial model, consider the position of the landlord, who generally needs to lease space. The worst situation for landlords is vacant real estate. You can largely determine the needs of the landlord's economic model by knowing the market. Ask your Realtor for sales per square foot and traffic comparisons for similar facilities. Traffic is a big part of what you are paying for, and rental rates should reflect any discrepancy in traffic. If your model requires sales of $500 per square foot but the facility averages sales of $250 per square foot, be cautious. The Cheesecake Factory can double the sales of its neighbors, but don't expect your performance to be this robust. As an operator, you have the job of not driving traffic to another facility. Your job is to attract that facility's traffic to your restaurant.

Next, interview current tenants. People love to talk and get a chance to tell their stories. Don't take this opportunity to tell your story—just listen carefully. Attempt to identify the risks. Ask the current tenants these questions:

- Which businesses are doing well in the facility (assuming a mall or similar type of real estate)? Why?
- How responsive is the landlord when you need help?
- Has the landlord fulfilled the promises he or she made prior to lease signing?
- What are the landlord's fears for the business at this location?

Your goal is to get the landlord to commit to realistic but favorable terms. You also want the comfort of knowing the landlord will honor his or her commitments. Take notes so you can refer back to exactly what was said and when. Be sure to view the deal in its entirety rather than term by term. Lease negotiation is not match play. Winning four of five conditions is not sufficient. You must win overall. Leave tenant improvement as the final component. Show the landlord your plans in a well-crafted memorandum and discuss your fine track record (see Figure 15.1). Let the landlord talk. Let the landlord sell. It is at this stage that the landlord is most likely to make a mistake. Find out how the landlord intends to deliver the property. Expect the landlord to lowball the proposed TI. Further, the landlord will try to include as tenant improvement such items as pulling all wires to your wall. A landlord should always pull the wires for the tenant; doing so is standard practice, not a concession.

You must ask these questions:

- Is the property separately metered; if not, will the landlord pay for the new meters?

FIGURE 15.1 Landlord Presentation

#	SECTION	DESCRIPTION
1	Executive Summary	One-page summary outlining the concept, the real estate strategy, and key management's background
2	Concept Description	Detailed description of the theme, menu, décor, and atmosphere
3	Location Analysis	Outline key real estate elements required for your business's success. For instance, traffic needs? Home or work side of the road? Mall?
4	Competitive Analysis	Your competition and their estimated economic performance
5	Marketing Plan	Outline how you will make the public aware of your business. Advertising? Advertising with discounting? Guerilla marketing? Publicist? Public relations firm?
6	Critical Success Factors	Outline the key factors necessary for your business's success? A slowing or growing economy? A strong review? Continued growth in a local development?
7	Management Bios	Provide résumés or bios that show you and your team belong in this business.
8	Press or Media Coverage of Past Projects	Provide press from past businesses. Good reviews are ideal.

- In what condition will the unit be delivered? Will the landlord pull the wires, including the phone on your wall?
- Are there co-op dollars available? Large malls have a marketing budget and often share marketing expenses with tenants.
- What are the average sales per square foot in the facility?
- Is the facility generating positive or negative comparable sales year over year?
- What is the landlord's greatest complaint about current tenants?
- What does the landlord think is the greatest complaint that the tenants have concerning the landlord?
- What is the occupancy rate for the facility?
- What is the average life of a business in the facility?
- What are the traffic counts by day?

Ideally, the landlord will determine from your line of questioning that you are sophisticated in lease negotiations and have done your homework. Next ask:

- How does the landlord think your business will perform in his or her facility?
- Why does the landlord think that your concept is a good fit for the facility?
- What amount of TI dollars is the landlord giving his or her restaurants?
- How many months of rent abatement has the landlord given other tenants?

Asking about other tenants puts the landlord on the spot. You're not asking what the landlord will give you; you're asking what the landlord has given others. The landlord knows that tenants talk and therefore may believe that it is not worth lying so will give valuable information. Anyway, you have already garnered these data.

If you believe in the location, counter his lowball TI offer. Tie your counteroffer to the strength of your concept. My partner, Scott

Condon, is the best I have ever seen at doing this. He has a background in real estate development and tremendous experience in deal negotiations. He is a formidable opponent for any landlord. The landlord must believe that your concept will not only pay the rent or the rent price you offer but drive traffic for the other tenants. Driving traffic for the facility is something you should be paid for. TI is an attractive method of payment, so tell the landlord that you need tenant improvement dollars. The question then is how much. The answer is where your needs intersect with the landlord's eagerness to have you as a tenant. You increase your chances of success by knowing this answer before posing the question.

16

THE GUARANTEE

Get it in writing.

As I previously indicated, you and your landlord are adversaries. This is not to say that your relationship cannot be professional, but simply that your interests are opposed, making you adversaries by definition if not behavior. Your landlord's objective is to rent space and collect your rent (as well as your common area maintenance fees). In addition, the landlord will want you to drive traffic for the other tenants and achieve a strong enough top line to ensure his or her participation in percentage rent. In sum, the landlord wants to negotiate risk out of the deal. By trying to reduce his or her risk, your landlord is asking you to accept more.

There are two types of risks: systematic risk and unsystematic risk. Systematic risk is the risk imbedded within the company and the industry. Unsystematic risk is market risk. Neither you nor your landlord can do much to combat market risk.

The personal guarantee is an important element of your landlord's risk-free investment strategy. The landlord will want you or one of your high-net-worth investors to guarantee the lease. In the event you close your business, you will still be required to pay rent unless and until the landlord elects to lease the property to another tenant. I do not believe in guarantees as a commercial concept. Purveyors, investors, and landlords all want guarantees. I work on the basis of best efforts. In the event the business goes as planned, we all make money. In the event that business faces challenges and underperforms, I expect everyone to behave as adults. Nevertheless, guarantees are commonly requested, and we must confront the topic.

If you have reached the lease negotiation phase of development, you may have more leverage than you think. You certainly have more bargaining power than you believe the landlord has. If you are neither an industry superstar nor a publicly traded restaurant company and a landlord is negotiating with you, it is fair to assume that the landlord has few options. Therefore, you can take a strong position on the subject of your personal guarantee.

Look at the situation this way: Restaurateurs often select a well-located space that needs improved infrastructure—plumbing, electrical, and the like. The upgrades are intended to increase the likelihood of your business's success over time. However, the upgrades increase the value of the landlord's property immediately. Therefore, why would you sign a guarantee? You have already paid compensation.

In addition, the lessee bears risk in the proposed relationship. The landlord's performance is a significant unknown for your enterprise to consider. I classify this risk as unsystematic, similar to the economy. In signing a lease, you are betting on the landlord's space and ability to maintain and promote it. The landlord's decisions and actions can have a material affect on your top line because of his or her influence and control over tenant mix, promotions, and upkeep. Your goal is to negotiate your risk out of the deal and leave the landlord with more.

When I discuss a guarantee with a landlord, I begin by accepting the premise that the lease will include a personal guarantee. However, I ask for a guarantee of my own. Remember that your success is dependent on the landlord's fulfilling the promises of his or her sales pitch. Remember, too, that you will likely be physically improving the property before you have a chance to open for business. In my counteroffer, I ask the landlord to guarantee my business a certain traffic rate and a 95 percent occupancy rate for the facility. Further, I require traffic to increase at my revenue growth rate. Clearly, my offer is fair, though I know that the landlord will not appreciate my proposal. No landlord likes to be held to his word.

Recently, my partner and I were negotiating with a landlord who, in an effort to get us to sign the lease, offered to pay for one-half of our advertising so long as we mentioned his facility. He said there was a co-op program in place that would match funds, with the only stipulation being he would have final approval of all ads. Once the lease was executed, we immediately attempted to participate in the co-op's advertising program. Every time we attempted to receive matching funds, the landlord found a reason to deny our marketing team the promised dollars. He asked that we change our tag line, he didn't like the advertising layouts, he didn't like the advertising venues—in short, he did everything he could do so as not to do what he said he would do. But why should I be the only party in the contract that is bound to deliver on his promises?

Now you have reached stalemate. Your gambit of agreeing to a guarantee (though asking for one in return) will make you appear reasonable. Continue by asking your potential landlord what he or she is attempting to accomplish with the guarantee. Invariably, you will be told that the landlord doesn't want you to operate a business in his or her facility without paying rent. This concern is reasonable and finds a fair solution in a "good-guy clause."

A *good-guy clause* is the answer to personal guarantees in New York. Rents are so high there that virtually no one can guarantee a lease. A good-guy clause states that you will personally guarantee the lease until you return the keys. In the event that your business is not profitable, you can attempt to assign the lease and sell the assets to another operator, liquidate the assets, or turn over the keys and leave the assets with the landlord. While you are determining your best course of action, you continue to pay rent—if not from operations then from your own pocket (personal guarantee). Once you have returned the keys, the property is the landlord's problem—or the opportunity of a lifetime if he recalls his marketing material. Obviously, if your business goes according to plan, the good-guy clause won't be an issue; but in the event that it fails, a good-guy clause allows you to stop your losses.

In explaining why they require a guarantee, landlords probably add that they want you to pay for them to lease the space to another tenant—a market-driven issue. Specifically, landlords who have maintained a property and marketed the facility correctly are able to lease the space quickly—maybe even at a higher rate than you paid. They may claim they require insurance against having to re-lease the property at a lower rent. That is, they want you to pay for an unsystematic risk—the risk of deflation.

Remind landlords like this about the other side of that coin: the risk you face of having to pay higher rent in a comparable facility—the risk of inflation. Lessees suffer and lessors prosper when vacancies arise in an environment of property inflation. The risk to landlords during deflation is vacancy. If they haven't upheld their bargain, of course no compensation is merited. A cause does exist if your restaurant fails in an otherwise thriving retail facility, a risk already reflected in the market rent. Further assurance, in terms of a guarantee, is superfluous. In any case, your uncompensated risk of property inflation surely outweighs a landlord's risk of property deflation.

RAISING CAPITAL

17

FINANCIAL MODELING

Modeling is the key to planning.

Much of our pursuit is quantitative and requires detailed, accurate financial analysis. I want to introduce the basics of financial modeling here, because we use this framework and these tools frequently through the end of the book.

This model is for nonaccountants. Eventually, a balance sheet will be necessary, but at this juncture the balance sheet is omitted. Also, the cash flow statement includes only net income, capital expenditures, and cash flow from financing. (See Chapters 19 and 22 for more on cash flow statements.) Later, your accountant will generate a complete set of financial projections for the undertaking.

BUILDING THE MODEL

Your financial model should include the following items:

- Revenue driver
- Income statements

- Cash flow statement
- Schedule of labor expenses

Revenue Driver

You have four methods from which to choose in building your revenue driver: (1) traffic and check average, (2) sales per square foot, (3) sales per seat, or (4) an average of the first three methods. In my opinion, traffic and check average are the most accurate and, it's hoped, are also the basis for your operating budget as well as establishing a useful projected-versus-actual variance to track.

If your concept is new, I suggest that you project revenue per day for one quarter. Project monthly revenue for the next nine months and annual revenue for the following four years. This procedure yields five years of projections. The first three months are critical and the most difficult to budget because you don't have an operating history. Your best guess is not very accurate and cash is tight. Daily projections help avoid pitfalls by more accurately forecasting cash.

Entrepreneurs often fail to disaggregate their projections. You, as an entrepreneur, may forecast $5 million per year of revenue. Based on concept, location, square footage, and so on, this may appear reasonable. However, you probably don't expect to generate $14,000 in the first day, $96,000 in the first week, and $413,000 in the first month. Daily projections allow you to account for holidays and one-time events that affect cash. Figures 17.1 through 17.4 illustrate revenue projections for the first month based on traffic and check average by day part (lunch, dinner, for example) for a 6,000-square-foot casual-dining restaurant opening on July 1.

Week 1 (Figure 17.1) included two promotional events and a holiday and generated $14,200. Figures 17.2 and 17.3 project revenue with only two of three possible revenue streams online. Lunch service, the third revenue stream, began in week 4 (Figure 17.4).

FIGURE 17.1 Revenue Driver—Week 1

XYZ RESTAURANT
PROJECTED REVENUE
FOR THE DAYS ENDING . . .

	1-Jul[a]	2-Jul[b]	3-Jul[c]	4-Jul[d]	5-Jul	6-Jul	7-Jul	Week 1
Lunch:								
Traffic	—	—	—	—	—	—	—	—
Check Average	$ 12	$ 12	$ 12	$ 12	$ 12	$ 12	$ 12	$ 12
Total Lunch Sales	$ —	$ —	$ —	$ —	$ —	$ —	$ —	$ —
Dinner:								
Traffic	—	—	75	—	125	150	200	550
Check Average	$ 16	$ 16	$ 16	$ 16	$ 16	$ 16	$ 16	$ 16
Total Dinner Sales	$ —	$ —	$ 1,200	$ —	$ 2,000	$ 2,400	$ 3,200	$ 8,800
Bar:								
Traffic	50	50	100	—	125	150	200	675
Check Average	$ 8	$ 8	$ 8	$ 8	$ 8	$ 8	$ 8	$ 8
Total Bar Sales	$ 400	$ 400	$ 800	$ —	$ 1,000	$ 1,200	$ 1,600	$ 5,400
Total Sales	$ 400	$ 400	$ 2,000	$ —	$ 3,000	$ 3,600	$ 4,800	$ 14,200

[a] Promotional Night
[b] Promotional Night
[c] Opening Night
[d] Closed for Holiday

FIGURE 17.2 Revenue Driver—Week 2

XYZ RESTAURANT
PROJECTED REVENUE
FOR THE DAYS ENDING . . .

	8-Jul	9-Jul	10-Jul	11-Jul	12-Jul	13-Jul	14-Jul	Week 2
Lunch:								
Traffic	—	—	—	—	—	—	—	—
Check Average	$ 12	$ 12	$ 12	$ 12	$ 12	$ 12	$ 12	$ 12
Total Lunch Sales	$ —	$ —	$ —	$ —	$ —	$ —	$ —	$ —
Dinner:								
Traffic	150	150	150	150	150	200	250	1,200
Check Average	$ 16	$ 16	$ 16	$ 16	$ 16	$ 16	$ 16	$ 16
Total Dinner Sales	$ 2,400	$ 2,400	$ 2,400	$ 2,400	$ 2,400	$ 3,200	$ 4,000	$ 19,200
Bar:								
Traffic	200	200	200	200	200	200	200	1,400
Check Average	$ 8	$ 8	$ 8	$ 8	$ 8	$ 8	$ 8	$ 8
Total Bar Sales	$ 1,600	$ 1,600	$ 1,600	$ 1,600	$ 1,600	$ 1,600	$ 1,600	$ 11,200
Total Sales	$ 4,000	$ 4,000	$ 4,000	$ 4,000	$ 4,000	$ 4,800	$ 5,600	$ 30,400

FIGURE 17.3 Revenue Driver—Week 3

XYZ RESTAURANT
PROJECTED REVENUE
FOR THE DAYS ENDING . . .

	15-Jul	16-Jul	17-Jul	18-Jul	19-Jul	20-Jul	21-Jul	Week 3
Lunch:								
Traffic	—	—	—	—	—	—	—	—
Check Average	$ 12	$ 12	$ 12	$ 12	$ 12	$ 12	$ 12	$ 12
Total Lunch Sales	$ —	$ —	$ —	$ —	$ —	$ —	$ —	$ —
Dinner:								
Traffic	300	300	300	300	300	400	400	2,300
Check Average	$ 16	$ 16	$ 16	$ 16	$ 16	$ 16	$ 16	$ 16
Total Dinner Sales	$ 4,800	$ 4,800	$ 4,800	$ 4,800	$ 4,800	$ 6,400	$ 6,400	$ 36,800
Bar:								
Traffic	200	200	200	200	200	200	200	1,400
Check Average	$ 8	$ 8	$ 8	$ 8	$ 8	$ 8	$ 8	$ 8
Total Bar Sales	$ 1,600	$ 1,600	$ 1,600	$ 1,600	$ 1,600	$ 1,600	$ 1,600	$ 11,200
Total Sales	$ 6,400	$ 6,400	$ 6,400	$ 6,400	$ 6,400	$ 8,000	$ 8,000	$ 48,000

FIGURE 17.4 Revenue Driver—Week 4

XYZ RESTAURANT
PROJECTED REVENUE
FOR THE DAYS ENDING . . .

	22-Jul	23-Jul	24-Jul	25-Jul	26-Jul	27-Jul	28-Jul	Week 4
Lunch:								
Traffic	200	200	200	200	300	300	200	1,600
Check Average	12	12	12	12	12	12	12	12
Total Lunch Sales	$ 2,400	$ 2,400	$ 2,400	$ 2,400	$ 3,600	$ 3,600	$ 2,400	$ 19,200
Dinner:								
Traffic	300	300	300	300	300	400	400	2,300
Check Average	16	16	16	16	16	16	16	16
Total Dinner Sales	$ 4,800	$ 4,800	$ 4,800	$ 4,800	$ 4,800	$ 6,400	$ 6,400	$ 36,800
Bar:								
Traffic	200	200	200	200	200	200	200	1,400
Check Average	8	8	8	8	8	8	8	8
Total Bar Sales	$ 1,600	$ 1,600	$ 1,600	$ 1,600	$ 1,600	$ 1,600	$ 1,600	$ 11,200
Total Sales	$ 8,800	$ 8,800	$ 8,800	$ 8,800	$ 10,000	$ 11,600	$ 10,400	$ 67,200

The first four weeks of revenue generated $159,800 in sales, well below the $400,000 needed to make a $5 million run rate. It will take a while for the business's marketing plan to fully reach the restaurant's customer base and for average weekly sales to reach $96,000.

Income Statements

I suggest that you produce monthly income statements for the first year and annual statements for the next four years. Begin with some broad guidelines. Assume that your casual-dining restaurant will have 33 percent food cost and 25 percent beverage cost. Lunch and dinner checks should be around 80 percent food and 20 percent beverage; the bar check is assumed to be 100 percent beverage. Assume the final three days of July average $9,000 per day, so the month of July closes with sales of $186,800. Operating expenses, which include rent, marketing, utilities, repairs, maintenance, linen, and cleaning supplies, are projected to be 27 percent of sales.

Before completing our Income Statement, we have to produce a Schedule of Labor Expense. Most models project labor as a percentage of total sales, but I find this method highly inaccurate. I view the majority of labor as a fixed expense. A restaurant needs the majority of its staff whether or not any customers are served. As a result, unpredictable sales generate high labor costs as a percentage of sales. Sending an hourly employee home can reduce labor only slightly. Therefore, I recommend treating labor as a fixed expense.

With the labor schedule complete, the entrepreneur's compensation is the only remaining piece to complete the monthly income statement. I return to this matter in Chapter 28, where deal structure is addressed. At this moment, you have the skills necessary to produce your financial statements.

FIGURE 17.5 Schedule of Labor Expense

XYZ RESTAURANT
PROJECTED ANNUAL SCHEDULES OF LABOR EXPENSE

	Per Hour	Hours Per Shift	Shifts Per Week	Salary	Total	%
Management:						
General Manager				$ 60,000		
Assistant Manager				40,000		
Assistant Manager				40,000		
Executive Chef				50,000		
Sous Chef				30,000		
Baker				30,000		
Total Management				$250,000	$250,000	22.1%
Front of the House:						
Hostess	$10.00	8	18	74,880		
Waiters	5.50	8	74	169,312		
Bussers	5.50	8	37	84,656		
Runners	5.50	8	29	66,352		
Coffee	5.50	8	7	16,016		
Bartenders	5.50	8	18	41,184		
Bar Backs	5.50	8	7	16,016		
Cocktail Waitresses	5.50	8	14	32,032		
Total Front of the House		64	204	$500,448	$500,448	44.3%
Kitchen:						
Cooks	10.00	8	28	116,480		
Prep Cooks	8.00	8	18	59,904		
Baking Assistants	10.00	8	14	58,240		
Dishwashers	7.00	8	14	40,768		
Receiver	12.00	8	5	24,960		
Porters	8.00	8	14	46,592		
Total Kitchen		48	93	$346,944	$346,944	30.7%
Administrative:						
Bookkeeper			5	32,000		
Total Administrative		–	5	$ 32,000	$ 32,000	2.8%
Total Labor Expense					$1,129,392	100.0%

18

FEW INVESTORS VERSUS MANY INVESTORS

*Investors should be considered a marketing tool
as well as your access to capital.*

Opening a restaurant requires a significant amount of capital. I believe it is better most often to have a group of investors rather than a single investor. With a group of investors, the success or failure of the business is shared among many. The entrepreneur's freedom of action and likelihood of success are enhanced when dealing with more than one investor.

Most entrepreneurs want to identify a single investor with whom they can grow. The logic is that each investor is a potential headache. Each investor and his or her spouse will have ideas and complaints that entrepreneurs believe will distract them from their duties. Furthermore, entrepreneurs believe that each investor is an additional potential lawsuit if the business doesn't meet its projections. All these fears are warranted. However, I believe that the additional challenges in managing a large investment group are well worth the effort. The single-investor model probably means that an entrepreneur's financial partner will have a lot of eggs in one basket. There is no such thing as a silent partner in the one-investor model.

Assemble the investor group carefully, strategically, and selectively. Recognize that anytime an investor has a great deal of money at stake, that investor is more likely to micromanage the project. In assembling your investment group, segment potential investors according to their industry and background. If possible, don't compile an investment group that represents only one industry. Attempt to assemble an investment group that represents marketing/advertising, finance, and manufacturing, similar to the way you would form a board of directors. The diversity will prove an asset.

I submit that each investor is not only a source of capital but of *feedback, ideas, customers,* and *publicity.* The restaurant industry is highly competitive. Raising the capital and building the unit are substantial hurdles. But the greatest challenge a restaurateur faces is putting people in the seats. Each investor is a marketing agent and a source of feedback from a target customer group.

Also, just as it is important for an investor to diversify his or her investment portfolio, it is important for an entrepreneur to limit the significance of the investment made by any individual. Otherwise, an unforeseen business challenge or even a personal issue could result in the exit of 100 percent of your capital. We'll look at a few scenarios.

Let's examine a $2 million restaurant project. Suppose you raised 100 percent of the capital from a single individual. Recognizing that $2 million is a great deal of money for a lone investor, this investor asks for frequent and detailed updates. Expect that any delay in the project will lead to a restatement of the investor's projections and returns. In the event that you fall short of your projections soon after opening, the $2 million investor has to constantly evaluate his or her opportunities. Specifically, is the project doomed or will the restaurant catch on? When should the investor attempt to force a sale just to get a portion of the $2 million investment back? What is the value of the assets and the lease? These are questions that will arise if the enterprise has a slow start.

Returns are always a critical issue in an investment. Preservation of capital assumes a larger role when the investor has risked too great a portion of his or her own wealth. An investment that projects a 25 percent internal rate of return (IRR) on a $2 million investment will pay the investor $500,000 per year interest for five years plus principal in the final year (see Figure 18.1). The principal payment can be the result of either a sale or a recapitalization.

Internal Rate of Return (IRR)

The interest rate that makes net present value of all cash flow equal zero.

Figure 18.2 assumes that the project begins more slowly than expected. In Year 1 the investor receives no distribution, and in Year 2 and Year 3 receives 50 percent of his or her expectation. Let's assume that an underperforming project cannot be sold at a premium or be recapitalized. Therefore, in Year 5 the investor will not receive his or her principal payment. Even if the investor receives payments of $500,000 through Year 10, the investor will receive only a 12 percent IRR. A 12 percent IRR is less than half the original expectation and is a poor return considering the risk.

FIGURE 18.1 Example of Returns Equaling a 25 Percent IRR

	YEAR 0	YEAR 1	YEAR 2	YEAR 3
Investment	$(2,000,000)	$ –	$ –	$ –
Cash Flow Distribution	–	500,000	500,000	500,000
Pro Rata Proceeds from a Sale	–	–	–	–
Total Stream of Cash Flow to Investor	$(2,000,000)	$ 500,000	$ 500,000	$ 500,000

	YEAR 4	YEAR 5	TOTAL
Investment	$ –	$ –	$(2,000,000)
Cash Flow Distribution	500,000	500,000	2,500,000
Pro Rata Proceeds from a Sale	–	2,000,000	2,000,000
Total Stream of Cash Flow to Investor	$ 500,000	$2,500,000	$ 2,500,000
Internal Rate of Return	25%		

FIGURE 18.2 Example of Returns If the Business Faces Early Challenges

	YEAR 0	YEAR 1	YEAR 2	YEAR 3	YEAR 4	YEAR 5
Investment	$(2,000,000)	$ —	$ —	$ —	$ —	$ —
Cash Flow Distribution	—	—	250,000	250,000	500,000	500,000
Pro Rata Proceeds from a Sale	—	—	—	—	—	—
Total Stream of Cash Flow to Investor	$(2,000,000)	$ —	$ 250,000	$ 250,000	$ 500,000	$ 500,000

	YEAR 6	YEAR 7	YEAR 8	YEAR 9	YEAR 10	TOTAL
Investment	$ —	$ —	$ —	$ —	$ —	$(2,000,000)
Cash Flow Distribution	500,000	500,000	500,000	500,000	500,000	4,000,000
Pro Rata Proceeds from a Sale	—	—	—	—	—	—
Total Stream of Cash Flow to Investor	$ 500,000	$ 500,000	$ 500,000	$ 500,000	$ 500,000	$ 2,000,000

Internal Rate of Return   12%

Perhaps the best strategy for the investor, assuming the asset is worth $1.5 million, is to force a sale in Year 3 (see Figure 18.3). The investor will have a 0 percent IRR after three years, but investment will have been returned and the investor can attempt to identify a more lucrative investment. Again, this problem is more pronounced if the investor has too many eggs in one basket.

Assume that you have assembled an investment group with 20 investors. Each investor purchases $100,000 of equity. Figure 18.4 illustrates the expectations of your hypothetical multi-investor group.

FIGURE 18.3 Example of Returns after a Forced Sale

	YEAR 0	YEAR 1	YEAR 2	YEAR 3
Investment	$(2,000,000)	$ –	$ –	$ –
Cash Flow Distribution	–	–	250,000	250,000
Pro Rata Proceeds from a Sale	–	–	–	1,500,000
Total Stream of Cash Flow to Investor	$(2,000,000)	$ –	$ 250,000	$1,750,000
Internal Rate of Return	0%			

FIGURE 18.4 Example of Returns Equaling a 25 Percent IRR

	YEAR 0	YEAR 1	YEAR 2
Investment	$(100,000)	$ –	$ –
Cash Flow Distribution	–	25,000	25,000
Pro Rata Proceeds from a Sale	–	–	–
Total Stream of Cash Flow to Investor	$(100,000)	$ 25,000	$ 25,000

	YEAR 3	YEAR 4	YEAR 5
Investment	$ –	$ –	$ –
Cash Flow Distribution	25,000	25,000	25,000
Pro Rata Proceeds from a Sale	–	–	100,000
Total Stream of Cash Flow to Investor	$ 25,000	$ 25,000	$ 125,000
Internal Rate of Return	25.0%		

Just as in our single-investor example, the multi-investor group expects a 25 percent internal rate of return. Figure 18.5 illustrates the returns these investors will receive if your project funded by our multi-investor group encounters the same problems as the single investor encountered.

The question is: Will your multi-investor group react to a decrease in its IRR as did your single investor? I believe the answer is no. Forcing a sale can be expensive. An investor may incur more than $75,000 in legal fees, wiping out any proceeds that he or she would have received. Also, the multi-investor group could band together to speak with a single voice, but organizing in this way is time consuming and unlikely.

In conclusion, I believe that a multi-investor group is the optimal approach to funding your project. The upside that is related to sales and marketing as well as the more relaxed approach to returns far outweighs the additional time you will spend addressing investor relations–related issues.

FIGURE 18.5 Example of Returns If the Business Faces Early Challenges

	YEAR 0	YEAR 1	YEAR 2	YEAR 3	YEAR 4	YEAR 5	TOTAL
Investment	$(100,000)	—	—	—	—	—	$(100,000)
Cash Flow Distribution	—	—	12,500	12,500	25,000	25,000	75,000
Pro Rata Proceeds from a Sale	—	—	—	—	—	—	—
Total Stream of Cash Flow to Investor	$(100,000)	$ —	$ 12,500	$ 12,500	$ 25,000	$ 25,000	$ (25,000)

	YEAR 6	YEAR 7	YEAR 8	YEAR 9	YEAR 10
Investment	—	—	—	—	—
Cash Flow Distribution	25,000	25,000	25,000	25,000	25,000
Pro Rata Proceeds from a Sale	—	—	—	—	—
Total Stream of Cash Flow to Investor	$ 25,000	$ 25,000	$ 25,000	$ 25,000	$ 25,000

Internal Rate of Return 12%

FIGURE 18.6 Example of Returns after a Forced Sale

	YEAR 0	YEAR 1	YEAR 2	YEAR 3	TOTAL
Investment	$(100,000)	$ –	$ –	$ –	$(100,000)
Cash Flow Distribution	–	–	12,500	12,500	25,000
Pro Rata Proceeds from a Sale	–	–	–	75,000	75,000
Total Stream of Cash Flow to Investor	$(100,000)	$ –	$ 12,500	$ 87,500	$ –

Internal Rate of Return   [0.0%]

19

DEBT VERSUS EQUITY

Don't be greedy in your first deals.

The mix of debt and equity is another consideration in deal structuring. Traditionally, commercial debt has not been available to restaurants, so the debt versus equity decision applied only to capital raised from investors. Assuming you are launching an independent restaurant, the key takeaway from this chapter is that a deal structured with debt is cheaper but the risk increases dramatically. With respect to small, private deals, most investors won't contribute capital in the form of debt. For this sort of investment, debt and equity have virtually the same legal position, but only equity will share the upside of success.

When a restaurant files for Chapter 7 bankruptcy, employees are paid first, tax collection agencies are paid second, purveyors are paid third, and lenders are paid fourth. Lenders have only a priority position over the equity holders or perhaps other lenders. However, an independent restaurant deal will be unlikely to have more than one tranche of debt, so in practice priority is over only equity holders. When a restaurant files for bankruptcy, it is fair to assume that very little money is available to distribute, perhaps not enough to satisfy the claims of employees and purveyors. Therefore, the creditors' claims to noncash assets represent their only realistic hope of recovering their investment. Unfortunately, assuming the property is leased, the value of restaurant assets generally amount to $0.10 for each dollar of debt. In short, debt holders have the downside of the equity holders without the equity holders' upside.

DEBT: THE POSITIVES

Figure 19.1 is an income statement from XYZ restaurant, which is financed with debt. In our example, the debt carries an interest rate of 10 percent and a term of five years (see Figure 19.2). The entrepreneur pays annual interest to his or her private lending group in the amount of $150,000 in Year 1, declining to $110,000 in Year 5. In this example, the entrepreneur owns 100 percent of cash flow. Prior to cash flow distribution, the entrepreneur must both make an allowance for capital improvements and make the principal on the debt (see Figure 19.3).

Now let's assume that restaurant XYZ was financed with equity (see Figure 19.4). The entrepreneur will not make any interest or principal payments, but the investors require a 25 percent IRR on a $500,000 investment. This amounts to 46 percent of the cash flow distributions (see Figures 19.5 and 19.6). Figure 19.7 compares the distributions to the entrepreneur in the debt scenario and the equity scenario.

In aggregate, the entrepreneur will receive 32 percent more cash by financing the restaurant with debt. In almost every instance, debt is less expensive than equity.

FIGURE 19.1 Debt Scenario: Projected Income Statement, 100 Percent Debt Financing

XYZ RESTAURANT
PROJECTED INCOME STATEMENTS
FOR THE YEARS ENDING . . .

	Year 1	Year 2	Year 3	Year 4	Year 5
Sales	$3,000,000	$3,300,000	$3,630,000	$3,993,000	$4,392,300
Cost of Sales	750,000	825,000	907,500	998,250	1,098,075
Gross Profit	2,250,000	2,475,000	2,722,500	2,994,750	3,294,225
Labor Expense	900,000	990,000	1,089,000	1,197,900	1,317,690
Operating Expense	750,000	825,000	907,500	998,250	1,098,075
Interest Expense	50,000	40,000	30,000	20,000	10,000
Pretax Income	550,000	620,000	696,000	778,600	868,460
Income Taxes	192,500	217,000	243,600	272,510	303,961
Net Income	$ 357,500	$ 403,000	$ 452,400	$ 506,090	$ 564,499
Cost Margins:					
Cost of Sales	25.0%	25.0%	25.0%	25.0%	25.0%
Labor Expense	30.0%	30.0%	30.0%	30.0%	30.0%
Operating Expense	25.0%	25.0%	25.0%	25.0%	25.0%
Profit Margins:					
Gross Profit	75.0%	75.0%	75.0%	75.0%	75.0%
Pretax Income	18.3%	18.8%	19.2%	19.5%	19.8%

FIGURE 19.2 Amortization Schedule

XYZ RESTAURANT
FIVE-YEAR AMORTIZATION SCHEDULE

Principal $ 500,000
Interest 10%
Years 5

Year	Principal	Payment	Interest	CUMULATIVE Interest	Principal	CUMULATIVE Principal
2004	$500,000	$(150,000)	$ 50,000	$ 50,000	$100,000	$100,000
2005	400,000	(140,000)	40,000	90,000	100,000	200,000
2006	300,000	(130,000)	30,000	120,000	100,000	300,000
2007	200,000	(120,0000)	20,000	140,000	100,000	400,000
2008	100,000	(110,000)	10,000	150,000	100,000	500,000

FIGURE 19.3 Debt Scenario: Cash Flow Distributions

XYZ RESTAURANT
PROJECTED DISTRIBUTION TABLE
FOR THE YEARS ENDING . . .

	Year 1	Year 2	Year 3	Year 4	Year 5
Cash Flow:					
Net Income	$ 357,500	$ 403,000	$ 452,400	$ 506,090	$ 564,499
Debt Payment	(100,000)	(100,000)	(100,000)	(100,000)	(100,000)
Capital Expenditures	(50,000)	(50,000)	(50,000)	(50,000)	(50,000)
Cash Flow for Distribution	$ 207,500	$ 253,000	$ 302,400	$ 356,090	$ 414,499

FIGURE 19.4 Equity Scenario: Projected Income Statement, 100% Equity Financing

XYZ RESTAURANT
PROJECTED INCOME STATEMENTS
FOR THE YEARS ENDING . . .

	Year 1	Year 2	Year 3	Year 4	Year 5
Sales	$3,000,000	$3,300,000	$3,630,000	$3,993,000	$4,392,300
Cost of Sales	750,000	825,000	907,500	998,250	1,098,075
Gross Profit	2,250,000	2,475,000	2,722,500	2,994,750	3,294,225
Labor Expense	900,000	990,000	1,089,000	1,197,900	1,317,690
Operating Expense	750,000	825,000	907,500	998,250	1,098,075
Interest Expense	—	—	—	—	—
Pretax Income	600,000	660,000	726,000	798,600	878,460
Income Taxes	210,000	231,000	254,100	279,510	307,461
Net Income	$ 390,000	$ 429,000	$ 471,900	$ 519,090	$ 570,999
Cost Margins:					
Cost of Sales	25.0%	25.0%	25.0%	25.0%	25.0%
Labor Expense	30.0%	30.0%	30.0%	30.0%	30.0%
Operating Expense	25.0%	25.0%	25.0%	25.0%	25.0%
Profit Margins:					
Gross Profit	75.0%	75.0%	75.0%	75.0%	75.0%
Pretax Income	20.0%	20.0%	20.0%	20.0%	20.0%

FIGURE 19.5 Equity Scenario: Cash Flow Distributions

XYZ RESTAURANT
PROJECTED CASH FLOW AND DISTRIBUTIONS
FOR THE YEARS ENDING . . . .

	Year 1	Year 2	Year 3	Year 4	Year 5	Total
Cash Flow:						
Net Income	$390,000	$429,000	$471,900	$519,090	$570,999	$2,380,989
Debt Payment	—	—	—	—	—	—
Capital Expenditures	(50,000)	(50,000)	(50,000)	(50,000)	(50,000)	(250,000)
Cash Flow for Distribution	$340,000	$379,000	$421,900	$469,090	$520,999	$2,130,989
Cash Flow Distribution:						
Entrepreneur	$185,300	$206,555	$229,936	$255,654	$283,944	$1,161,389
Investor Group	154,700	172,445	191,965	213,436	237,055	969,600
	$340,000	$379,000	$421,900	$469,090	$520,999	$2,130,989

FIGURE 19.6 Equity Scenario: Investor Group's IRR

XYZ RESTAURANT
INTERNAL RATE OF RETURN

	Year 0	Year 1	Year 2	Year 3	Year 4	Year 5	Total
Cash Flow Distribution:							
Investor Group	$(500,000)	$154,700	$172,445	$191,965	$213,436	$237,055	$969,600

IRR | 25% |

FIGURE 19.7 Comparison of Debt and Equity Scenarios

XYZ RESTAURANT
ENTREPRENEUR'S CASH FLOW DISTRIBUTION COMPARISON
FOR THE YEARS ENDING . . .

	Year 1	Year 2	Year 3
Cash Flow Distribution:			
100% Debt Financing	$ 207,5000	$ 253,000	$ 302,400
100% Equity Financing	185,300	206,555	229,936

	Year 4	Year 5	Total
Cash Flow Distribution:			
100% Debt Financing	$ 356,090	$ 414,499	$1,533,489
100% Equity Financing	255,654	283,944	1,161,389

DEBT: THE NEGATIVES

Debt financing can be complex and dangerous. Unlike equity, debt repayments are scheduled irrespective of the success of the enterprise. Debt is a significant fixed cost, which, when combined with rent, can be a very significant cash flow hurdle to clear each month. Depending on your loan covenants, tight cash flow can mean the end of your business as you know it. In simple terms, you have control of your business until you miss a payment. If you become in default, control of the business may transfer to creditors.

It has been my experience that rent payments in cities like New York that are based on long and expensive leases are difficult enough to make. From an operations perspective, debt payments divert valuable working capital from training programs, marketing, and other activities that give your business the best chance of success. My opinion is that debt is far too risky in the early stage of deals. Entrepreneurs do better to focus on driving the top line and cutting costs than they are making debt payments. Further, a well-thought-out investment group offers many opportunities when all parties' incentives in a deal are aligned. Debt holders don't have the same incentives as do equity holders.

20

PROFILING THE INVESTMENT GROUP

Precision is the key to success.

Raising capital is difficult even when undertaken appropriately. Most often an entrepreneur has the interests and background of an operator, but raising capital is a finance matter and well outside most entrepreneurs' comfort zone. The process of raising money can be excruciatingly painful. Beyond the general discomfort of turning up hat in hand to friends, family, and acquaintances, you'll be treated to a rough personal examination. Though difficult, this process is extremely useful. You'll be forced to tell your story almost endlessly. In being challenged on the particulars of your business plan, you'll become more confident in some details and make improvements to others. The process requires sharp focus and organization but generally pays off—though sometimes the payoff is preventing you from losing money rather than giving you the opportunity to make it.

Most of the world never knows the trauma the majority of entrepreneurs go through in raising capital. Most people think that getting a mortgage loan is intrusive, but raising capital is exponentially worse. Not only must an investor be comfortable with your knowledge of the business but he or she must also know that you have the drive, perseverance, ethics, and character to generate a return on capital. The investor has only your projections and your history. The investor will look to see if you have been successful in the past, specifically trying to ascertain whether you know how to win.

The characteristics that make investors challenging are the same characteristics that make them savvy. The average investors see far more business plans than do the average entrepreneurs. Investors have seen the good, the bad, and the ugly and expect your plan and presentation to incorporate the best of what they have seen. It is this process that helps entrepreneurs identify critical success factors. Investors will challenge on the conceptual. For example, they want to know that you have identified your primary market and your secondary market and that the two markets will be approached differently. They will challenge on the mundane. For instance, how many cooks do you need per night, and what is the wage rate of the bartending staff? Overall, they want to determine whether you are experienced enough to not overreact to a bad week of sales. Can you deal with market changes—new entrants in the market, a downturn in the economy, or personal tragedy? Are you likely to treat the investors fairly when it comes to distributions or will you "cook the books"?

Not only is capital raising a difficult process but it is also time consuming. It consumes time when time is in short supply. If you are attempting to raise money for your first deal, you most likely have a full-time job. It is my experience that raising capital is the make-or-break stage of entrepreneurship—you will launch your concept if you raise the money. If you can't raise the money, the concept will end up as no more than another good idea in your top drawer. You may have a great plan and plenty of commitment, but after a few months of working eight-plus hours a day on your business and raising money in your free time, you'll begin to question your approach.

Further, raising capital can be expensive. For instance, an investor located many miles from you may suggest that you present your plan to his group. Yes, this could be a good opportunity but airfare adds up; so will your printing and binding costs preparing for the meeting. Therefore, it is critical that you think hard about raising the investment. You essentially have to treat raising capital as a separate business—and this business also requires a business plan.

Begin by creating an investor database. List every contact that may have the wherewithal to invest in your project (see Figure 20.1). Next, separate the database into three categories—most likely, worth a try, and unlikely (see Figure 20.2). Continue to fill in the database throughout the process as introductions and referrals arise. A few rules to follow:

- You will have greater success raising money from someone you know than from someone you don't know.
- You will have greater success raising money from someone who has had success in a project that you have been part

FIGURE 20.1 Investor Database

INVESTOR DATABASE					
Investor Name	E-mail Address	Phone	Relationship	Investor's Industry	Investor's Past Investments

FIGURE 20.2 Investor Database: By Category

INVESTOR DATABASE					
Group 1 - Most Likely					
Investor Name	E-mail Address	Phone	Relationship	Investor's Industry	Investor's Past Investments
Group 2 - Worth a Try					
Investor Name	E-mail Address	Phone	Relationship	Investor's Industry	Investor's Past Investments
Group 3 - Unlikely					
Investor Name	E-mail Address	Phone	Relationship	Investor's Industry	Investor's Past Investments

of, even if your part was small. You must be associated with
success.

- You will have greater success raising money from those who
don't work in the restaurant industry. Investors who have
achieved financial success in the industry may not think
they need you.
- You will have greater success raising money from those who
are customers of like concepts. Conversely, a potential investor who shares his delightful experiences at the Olive
Garden will not likely be an investor for a high-quality, high-
end restaurant.
- You will have greater success raising money from those who
are geographically proximate to the restaurant. Most investors in a single unit want to be patrons as well; the investment most likely is tied to their ego.
- You will have greater success raising money from those who
work in a creative or financial business. Most concrete man-
ufacturers, as an example, will have no interest in investing
in a restaurant and won't understand the business even if
they claim they do.
- You will have greater success raising money from those who
work in a high-margin industry. For instance, a general contractor works off tight margins and thus places too great a
value on a dollar to be an appropriate investor in a restaurant.
- You will have greater success raising money from someone
who has previously made high-risk investments. Don't spend
too much time courting an investor with an extensive bond
portfolio.

The pursuit of financing is so encompassing at times that entrepreneurs chase unlikely sources and divert their attention from
more appropriate concerns. Be careful of "tire kickers" and especially of those who fancy themselves financiers (more on this in
Chapter 23). They will waste the precious time that you should be

allocating toward more likely investors, human resources, operations, marketing plans, and the like.

A few years ago I worked with a friend on a high-end restaurant concept. He believed that the resurgence of Denver's downtown created a platform that would support a posh restaurant-lounge similar to those found in New York, Miami, and Los Angeles. Two attorneys approached my friend after learning about his plan. They wanted to raise the capital and perhaps even invest themselves. They claimed to know a network of high-net-worth individuals that would fly to Denver for a pitch. My friend and I arranged a meeting in a downtown Denver restaurant to interview the attorneys. I began with friendly questions. Where do you live? Where is your office? Had you ever been to this restaurant? My friend and I became very suspicious that they both lived and worked in Denver suburbs and seldom went downtown. They, in turn, asked how I liked living in New York. I responded favorably and asked when they had last been there. One responded many years ago; one said never. Neither had been to Los Angeles.

As the evening wore on, I became more certain that the two attorneys were wasting our time. In trying to sell their ability, they stated that they could introduce us to a local family in the concrete business. They also offered that once our projections were complete, they would introduce us to the local bank. High finance indeed.

I wondered how two guys without experience with similar restaurants, similar cities, or similar guests could sell the concept to an investor. I wondered what would make them think that (1) we needed an introduction to a bank and (2) a bank would invest in a start-up restaurant. The bank was out. The concrete family was out as well. The odds of an old-economy family investing in a start-up restaurant were so slim as to be nil. Of course, the attorneys were out.

Had we engaged the attorneys, we would have lost six months pursuing tire kickers. For them this was a part-time opportunity.

On the other hand, the project was a career for my friend and me. This was how we planned to raise our families and pay our bills. We were the only ones with something to lose.

Categorize your investor database using the guidance I provided in Figures 20.1 and 20.2. In the event that you are unsuccessful raising the capital in Group 1, ask yourself why. If qualified individuals who have an interest in similar risk investments pass on your deal, you have either a weak plan or a weak presentation. I would attempt to resolve these questions before pursuing Group 2. I would never pursue Group 3.

Unfortunately, this categorizing is a process that most of you cannot outsource. You may have associates who offer to raise the money for your deal for a percentage of the company or for a fee. Outsourcing will be successful only if you can't afford the time and will fail if you are incapable of completing the task yourself. Think of it in terms of getting a loan from a bank when you need money—impossible. I would never invest in a start-up if the entrepreneur were not leading the capital-raising effort. The message you would be sending your investors is that investor relations and investor capital is not your primary focus but rather a task like graphic design that you are outsourcing.

An entrepreneur's relationship with his or her investors is the most important relationship in start-up ventures. In the beginning, an investor is the entrepreneur's key customer, not the guest in the dining room. Once successful, the tables will turn. In many deals investors become a commodity and are lucky participants. With success, entrepreneurs can position their deals as "take it or leave it." Eventually, with success, money becomes less critical to deals—capital is abundantly available and sourcing good deals becomes the critical path.

Because deals have a limited shelf life, trying to outsource the task of raising capital is to guarantee failure. Entrepreneurs may require professional guidance in structuring a deal, but if entrepreneurs can't raise capital for their venture, then such entrepreneurs have no business leading a deal. Specifically, if you are attempting to launch a business, yet you have no relationships with individuals or financial institutions that have an interest in financing your deal, you will not have developed enough of a foundation in your industry to lead your deal. A chef or a general manager attempting to develop his or her first start-up venture should have developed relationships with guests and industry associates who can be "tapped" for seed funding. If not, then the chef or general manager has to develop those relationships before considering launching a first venture.

A few years ago I received a call from a guy in Chicago who had an idea. He believed that he had identified an underserved niche that, with my help, could be exploited. He stated that he was comfortable in operations but he needed an advisor and had to raise the money for his deal. Further, he explained that he had zero sources of capital. Think about it. What is he saying? How could he possibly have zero sources of capital if he were remotely qualified to do the deal he was outlining? He expected me to contact my relationships and ask them to put money into a deal I would not control, a deal led by a novice. Remember, whoever brings the money in a start-up venture controls the deal. The phone call had myriad problems: (1) The guy had no track record, just an idea; (2) it would take a long time before I would be comfortable being involved with someone with whom I had no relationship; and (3) Chicago is way too cold. The good news is that the phone call was short and he never called back.

I have raised capital for many small ventures, but they were ones in which the entrepreneur already had a track record. I have been successful in an agent's role only if the entrepreneur has a long list of interested parties with whom he or she has a relationship. You can't skip a step. Pursuing short cuts will always result in failure. In short, without a track record you have to raise the capital yourself.

21

THE REAL ESTATE APPROACH: PEOPLE ARE ASSETS

*Question: Who believes that a restaurant's value
is in its capital assets?*
Answer: A real estate investor.

My dealings with real estate investors regarding the restaurant industry have been entirely confusing. Typically, a real estate investor makes money trading capital assets. The assets can be easily valued, bought, and sold. A restaurant or restaurant company has hard assets, but the true value of the company is in the human assets—for example, the CEO, COO, CFO, general managers, and the systems for recruiting, training, motivating, measuring, and compensating them. The human assets run the company. The human assets are most often the difference between success and failure in a highly competitive industry. Location is a key driver of revenue, but guests are indifferent to a restaurant's buy-versus-lease policy. The guests' experience is what can turn a guest's initial patronage into an annuity stream; and the guests' experience turns more on the staff's execution of your business plan than on physical assets.

Ideally, you can fund your restaurant with enough capital to tend to every detail. However, capital is usually scarce and therefore allocated to the business's greatest need. I have found that independent restaurants are biased toward expenses, and restaurant chains are biased toward capital assets. In other words, restaurant chains typically take the approach of a real estate investor.

I cringe when I hear people state they are interested in buying a restaurant company because of the real estate value. This is not to say that money can't be made buying a restaurant for its real estate. But my experience with real estate investors at the helm is that operations suffer; and the suffering is most evident in employee turnover. Again, little value is placed on human assets.

Restaurateurs are not concerned with depreciation and asset value. A restaurateur is concerned with the guests' experience. To a restaurateur, cash is nothing more than cash. Cash spent on a training program is as important as cash spent on a new stove. To a real estate investor, cash spent on a training program is cash wasted; a training program is an operating expense and won't add to the book value of the company. I believe that a training program has a material effect on profit and is an essential part of the business. Everyone recognizes the importance of a stove to a restaurant. Only one other group values training the way that operators do: the customers.

It is difficult for a real estate investor to understand the importance of culture. Happy employees need to understand that their manager cares about them. My experience indicates it is impossible to convey to real estate investors the benefit of culture-building exercises. Real estate investors never show emotion, never are late to work, never get sick, and never ever have a family crisis.

22

THE APPLE DOES FALL FAR FROM THE TREE

One standard deviation may be
geometrically different.

A new entrepreneur could easily conclude that any financial partner is better than no financial partner. When an entrepreneur is desperate, money is coveted like oxygen. However, as we shall see, financial investors can be more trouble than they are worth.

When identifying potential financial partners, look for people with similar goals, particularly when you are beginning to craft your own deals. Generally, early in your deal-making career, your investors are more likely to be partners than to be silent investors. Financial contributors want greater control in the business when you don't have a positive track record. Once you have a record of success, however, you can dictate the terms of a deal on a take-it-or-leave-it basis. Therefore, it is critical that all directors have the same outlook toward work and success during each phase of the business. Otherwise, small changes in the business will result in larger problems.

New York City, a very interesting place, is the primary or secondary residence for many superwealthy people. I have often joked that in several of my partnership groups, I was the only person who didn't own an airplane. Instead of buying a plane, I elected to purchase shoes, electricity, and food. My business school program taught us to believe that being close to wealth is the first step toward creating wealth. Access to wealth may help create wealth; but I believe, more specifically, that close proximity to the originators of wealth is where opportunity lies. My experience is that the progeny of wealth are like old photocopies. The original is crisp but each successive copy fades and eventually becomes unrecognizable. I should say that I have had wonderful, competent partners who were very wealthy and came from wealthy families. You are probably wondering how this relates to raising capital for restaurants.

In New York you meet the son or daughter of seemingly every successful family in the world. Many of those sons or daughters are looking for direction or purpose in life. They often have a trust fund at their disposal. Inevitably, they have an epiphany, the result often being to ask, "Why not restaurants?" I have been in numerous meetings with the scions of wealth trying to value the capital as well as their family's contribution. Each sentence seems to begin with "My father will . . ." The implied promise is that the successful father is willing to take his focus from his core enterprise to help a restaurant that his son invested in. This offer is nice, if off point, until he reveals he intends to be paid for having a successful father. Early in my career I was influenced to the point that my salary and equity participation were affected.

Earlier in this book we established that most potential hires are full of baloney. This is true for investors looking for a preferred position based on factors other than risk and invested capital. Investor negotiations concerning future provision of value are problematic on two levels. First, investors attempting to get a more favorable equity allocation than their capital deserves reduce the financial benefit you'll receive. Second, those same investors get the opportunity to earn their "sweat equity" (a grandfather's sweat 50 years ago) after you've created the asset platform.

Figure 22.1 illustrates the problem. As an example, assume you are the entrepreneur and managing partner of a new business. In our first scenario (see Figure 22.1), the investment group negotiated a $600,000 investment based on an 18 percent hurdle rate. If your business generates $3 million per year in sales and has 12 percent cash flow margins, you'll have $360,000 of annual cash flow. Assume that each year your business will need capital improvements of $30,000, leaving $330,000 of distributable cash flow. Your investors require $108,000 annually (18 percent hurdle rate × $600,000 investment), leaving you with distributable funds of $220,000. Scenario 2 (see Figure 22.1) contains the same assumptions as Scenario 1 except that the cash flow assumption is now 15 percent versus 12 percent originally. Now the business has $90,000 of additional distributions available for the management team.

Scenario 3 (see Figure 22.2) illustrates the difference in annual cash flow distribution if management gives investors sweat equity. In Scenario 3, the investment group negotiated 70 percent of the business for a $600,000 investment. The equity percentage is based on the promise that the investment group will provide capital today

FIGURE 22.1 Distribution of Free Cash Flow: Scenarios 1 and 2

SCENARIO 1		SCENARIO 2	
Distribution of Free Cash Flow		**Distribution of Free Cash Flow**	
Revenue	$3,000,000	Revenue	$3,000,000
Cash Flow Margins	12%	Cash Flow Margins	15%
Cash Flow	$ 360,000	Cash Flow	$ 450,000
Capital Expenditures	30,000	Capital Expenditures	30,000
Distributable Cash Flow	330,000	Distributable Cash Flow	420,000
Invested Capital	600,000	Invested Capital	600,000
Hurdle Rate	18%	Hurdle Rate	18%
Required Return on Invested Capital	$ 108,000	Required Return on Invested Capital	$ 108,000
Investor Percentage of Distribution	33%	Investor Percentage of Distribution	26%
Management Percentage of Distribution	67%	Management Percentage of Distribution	74%
Cash Flow to Management	$ 222,000	Cash Flow to Management	$ 312,000

FIGURE 22.2 Distribution of Free Cash Flow: Scenarios 3 and 4

SCENARIO 3		SCENARIO 4	
Distribution of Free Cash Flow		**Distribution of Free Cash Flow**	
Revenue	$3,000,000	Revenue	$3,000,000
Cash Flow Margins	12.0%	Cash Flow Margins	15.0%
Cash Flow	$ 360,000	Cash Flow	$ 450,000
Capital Expenditures	30,000	Capital Expenditures	30,000
Distributable Cash Flow	330,000	Distributable Cash Flow	420,000
Hurdle Rate	na	Hurdle Rate	na
Invested Capital	600,000	Invested Capital	600,000
Required Return on		Required Return on	
Invested Capital	na	Invested Capital	na
Investor Percentage		Investor Percentage	
of Distribution	70.0%	of Distribution	70.0%
Cash Flow to		Cash Flow to	
Management	$ 231,000	Management	$ 294,000
Management Percentage		Management Percentage	
of Distribution	30.0%	of Distribution	30.0%
Cash Flow to		Cash Flow to	
Management	$ 99,000	Management	$ 126,000

as well as opportunities and capital in the future. The difference in cash flow to management (or the entrepreneur) between Scenario 1 and Scenario 3 is $123,000—enough for many pairs of shoes, maybe even a plane. This sum is a substantial exchange for the vague promise of future business.

If we keep the same assumptions in Scenario 4 as in Scenario 3 (see Figure 22.2) except for increasing the cash flow margins to 15 percent, negotiating on future value will create a loss for management of $186,000 annually.

The issue at hand is to properly value equity and an investor's claim to more than a pro rata share. If an investor invests money before lease signing or being fully funded, he or she may reasonably request a greater return on investment than an investor who places capital at a less risky juncture. The investors that I am wary (and weary) of are those who want to convince you that their worth goes far beyond money. If you develop a concept and are responsible for the results, all the success is most likely yours.

Be very careful about how much you pay for a promise. Face it; the odds of your restaurant succeeding are statistically slim. Ninety-five out of 100 restaurants fail within the first three years after opening. However, if you are successful, the world is your oyster. Many opportunities will present themselves. Therefore, why would you give an investor a more favorable equity allocation for what that investor will provide? Again, you won't need the previous promise of new deals if you succeed. But if you fail, be assured the promise won't be heeded. The argument is irrational, but I hear it often.

H *u r d l e*
R *a t e*

The minimum return an investor requires to make an investment at a given level of risk.

In the event that you have investors requiring an intrusive position in your first deal, remember it is important that you and your partners have similar goals for the business and similar goals for life. You may find that you have absentee partners with decision-making authority or partners who have less ambition than you do. It's a bad situation when you are hungrier than your partners are; and, further, you may create levels of bureaucracy that make decision making arduously slow.

23

THE TIRE KICKER

Time is of the essence.

If you are just beginning to create your own deals, it's critical that you apply the same cynicism to potential investors as you do to potential employees. If potential investors have too much available time, a limited track record in private equity, and a propensity to call meetings, they are likely to be tire kickers. Beware! These folk fill their days with your time.

If you have developed your concept, assembled your team, identified your location, crafted your model and your sales memorandum, then you have already invested a great deal of time and money in your project. You have arrived at the capital-raising phase, where deals are made and lost. You have a limited amount of time to secure financing or your deal will begin to unravel. The longer the funding process takes, the more likely you will lose key management and will become disheartened with the process. I have seen many great ideas come to an end during this phase.

The failure to raise funds for a legitimate business often results from a poorly managed capital-raising process. And without capital, the project will end up in the top drawer. The top drawer of my desk is the graveyard of abandoned entrepreneurial projects.

Your goal is to develop a group of investors who fund your current project and grow with you as you develop future projects. Your investment group should act as advisors, navigating you away from potential business land mines. Finally, your investment group should be capable of developing new opportunities. The difficult part of capital raising isn't pricing the deal but, rather, it's identifying investors worth pursuing. During my years as a chef I was often approached by the wrong kind of investor. You know the type—a restaurant patron who had sold a rental property for a capital gain of $12,000 or had closed a rather large Amway deal and was two scotches in. As are most young chefs, I was looking to open my own restaurant. I spent countless hours with patrons discussing my proposed project only to learn that they didn't have any money. I should have been angrier at the imposters at the time, but I figured that because I didn't have any money either, wasting my time was OK.

Ultimately, you want to develop a network of individual investors or investment funds you can go to for each of your projects. In developing that network, you want to avoid both individuals who falsely claim to be investors and tire kickers. As frustrating as it is to learn that the person who has been reviewing your project has no money, it is infuriating dealing with a tire kicker. A tire kicker is an individual who has money but is in the business of discussing deals. The tire kicker has all day to meet but gets cold feet when it comes time to write the check. The tire kicker's false bravado during calls and meetings masks his or her fear.

I found that I could quickly spot a tire kicker. The tire kicker

- is always available to meet during business hours;
- returns your phone calls immediately;
- wants to discuss your project as well as future projects; and
- never brings additional investors to look at your deal.

A proxy for an investor's level of interest is the degree that the investor is willing to extend himself or herself for your deal. For instance, if a qualified investor arranges a meeting with friends to meet you and view your deal, then that investor has extended himself tremendously. The quality of your presentation to the group will affect the investor's credibility with his or her peers. Tire kickers never bring potential coinvestors to your deal because they have no intention of investing in your deal—they simply have free time to kill and tell tales of the one that got away.

When developing your investment group, here are a few helpful reminders:

- Look for individuals, not companies. A restaurant deal is seldom appropriate for a business-to-business investment.
- Look for individuals who have a track record in private equity deals.
- Look for individuals who may benefit from a restaurant deal. Individuals who entertain for business may benefit from owning a restaurant because the venue becomes an extension of their office. Purveyors of specialty food may want to find a marquee location for introducing new products. Designers may want the opportunity to design a restaurant as a business calling card.

After generating a list of investor prospects, you can then develop your sales pitch. In your sales pitch, stress the strategic benefits of being involved in the deal. If you have a high-profile partner, talk to potential investors about the benefits of being in a deal with this partner and the ways you will facilitate doing business at your restaurant. Frame the opportunity as much more than a financial deal. All investors want their money back plus a return, but the successful deal needs more than the promise of financial gain. Maybe some investors' involvement in a deal increases deal flow for their business. Or maybe some investors anticipate being exposed to a social world they have had an interest in penetrating.

Regardless, most investors looking at a start-up have other more secure investment opportunities. To close a start-up restaurant deal, the story must position the deal beyond financial returns. In short, everyone wants to be part of something special, and it's your job to identify what is truly special about your deal.

Asking potential investors the hard questions on the first day is difficult for most entrepreneurs, particularly for those new to deal making. Early on, entrepreneurs behave as if they are there merely to answer questions, not to ask them. But once an entrepreneur gets in front of an individual with capital, the entrepreneur believes that so long as the lead is alive, there's a chance the project will get funded. Investors know very quickly whether a deal is interesting. Successful investors are used to asking hard questions and therefore don't mind answering hard questions. Spending time dealing with leads that don't pay is time better used to develop other sources of capital.

24

PROJECTIONS: HIGH, MEDIUM, OR LOW

Underpromise and overdeliver.

Entrepreneurs face a dilemma when deciding whether to present high, low, or medium projections to potential investors. If they provide aggressive projections, they are more likely to get their particular project funded but are also more likely to encounter shareholder disputes if the projections aren't met. If entrepreneurs provide low projections, they risk not getting funded.

I have lost investors many times to other opportunities because I presented conservative projections, and my competition presented what I thought were wildly optimistic projections. Average sales in the restaurant industry are approximately $400 per square foot. The Cheesecake Factory leads chain restaurants with sales of slightly less than $1,000 per square foot. Restaurants in highly populated areas can exceed $1,000 per square foot, but this level is improbable.

Let's examine a 5,000-square-foot restaurant venue being pursued by two entrepreneurs: Entrepreneur A and Entrepreneur B. Entrepreneur A is optimistic about his concept. He expects to have an average check of $25 and wants to have 100 seats. Figure 24.1 contains the projections that Entrepreneur A presents to his potential investor group. Entrepreneur B is more optimistic about her concept. She expects to have an average check of $40 and intends to have 150 seats. Figure 24.2 presents the projections Entrepreneur B shows to her potential investor group.

Assume that the potential investor group is looking to place $500,000 in an independent restaurant for 50 percent of the cash flow distributions. The group reviews Entrepreneur A's and Entrepreneurs B's projections. The potential investors, who may not be very savvy about the restaurant industry, may wonder why they would invest in Entrepreneur A's restaurant when Entrepreneur B's restaurant will be so much more successful. According to the projections, Entrepreneur B's project will generate a 77 percent IRR, whereas Entrepreneur A's project will generate a 34 percent IRR. Entrepreneur A's question is whether he did himself a disservice by presenting projections that he considered realistic but that underwhelmed the investment group?

In raising capital, competing against overly optimistic projections is a very real problem. Think back to the dot-com era. It was difficult to raise capital for a restaurant when investors were being presented with dot-com projections with geometric returns. In generating pro formas, I produce high, medium, and low projections. On one hand, high projections provide your deal the highest probability of being financed; investors are interested in the results of a home run project. On the other hand, low projections are appropriate because they reveal the minimum amount of revenue required to give investors a return on their investment.

Investors should learn from a close inspection that Entrepreneur B's projections are impossible to attain (see Figure 24.3).

Remember that the prospective location for Entrepreneur B's restaurant is 5,000 square feet. Therefore, Entrepreneur B will have to generate $1,200 sales per square foot—not impossible but unlikely. Further examination exposes the necessary table-turns to meet projections—6.6 per day in Year 1 and 9.7 per day in Year 5. If we

FIGURE 24.1 Entrepreneur A's Projected Income Statements

ENTREPRENEUR A—XYZ RESTAURANT
PROJECTED INCOME STATEMENTS FOR THE YEARS ENDING . . .

	Year 1	Year 2	Year 3	Year 4	Year 5
Sales	$ 3,500,000	$ 3,675,000	$ 3,858,750	$ 4,051,688	$ 4,254,272
Cost of Sales	875,000	918,750	964,688	1,012,922	1,063,568
Gross Profit	2,625,000	2,756,250	2,894,063	3,038,766	3,190,704
Labor Expense	1,050,000	1,102,500	1,157,625	1,215,506	1,276,282
Operating Expense	875,000	918,750	964,688	1,012,922	1,063,568
Pretax Income	700,000	735,000	771,750	810,338	850,854
Income Taxes	245,000	257,250	270,113	283,618	297,799
Net Income	$ 455,000	$ 477,750	$ 501,638	$ 526,719	$ 553,055
Cash Flow:					
Net Income	$ 455,000	$ 477,750	$ 501,638	$ 526,719	$ 553,055
Capital Expenditures	(50,000)	(50,000)	(50,000)	(50,000)	(50,000)
Cash Flow for Distribution	$ 405,000	$ 427,750	$ 451,638	$ 476,719	$ 503,055
Cost Margins:					
Cost of Sales	25.0%	25.0%	25.0%	25.0%	25.0%
Labor Expense	30.0%	30.0%	30.0%	30.0%	30.0%
Operating Expense	25.0%	25.0%	25.0%	25.0%	25.0%
Profit Margins:					
Gross Profit	75.0%	75.0%	75.0%	75.0%	75.0%
Pretax Income	20.0%	20.0%	20.0%	20.0%	20.0%
Net Income	13.0%	13.0%	13.0%	13.0%	13.0%
Unit Statistics:					
Square Footage	5,000	5,000	5,000	5,000	5,000
Seats	100	100	100	100	100
Check Average	$ 25	$ 25	$ 25	$ 25	$ 25

FIGURE 24.2 Entrepreneur B's Projected Income Statements

ENTREPRENEUR B—XYZ RESTAURANT
PROJECTED INCOME STATEMENTS FOR THE YEARS ENDING . . . .

	Year 1	Year 2	Year 3	Year 4	Year 5
Sales	$ 6,000,000	$ 6,600,000	$ 7,260,000	$ 7,986,000	$ 8,784,600
Cost of Sales	1,500,000	1,650,000	1,815,000	1,996,500	2,196,150
Gross Profit	4,500,000	4,950,000	5,445,000	5,989,500	6,588,450
Labor Expense	1,800,000	1,980,000	2,178,000	2,395,800	2,635,380
Operating Expense	1,500,000	1,650,000	1,815,000	1,996,500	2,196,150
Pretax Income	1,200,000	1,320,000	1,452,000	1,597,200	1,756,920
Income Taxes	420,000	462,000	508,200	559,020	614,922
Net Income	$ 780,000	$ 858,000	$ 943,800	$ 1,038,180	$ 1,141,998
Cash Flow:					
Net Income	$ 780,000	$ 858,000	$ 943,800	$ 1,038,180	$ 1,141,998
Capital Expenditures	(50,000)	(50,000)	(50,000)	(50,000)	(50,000)
Cash Flow for Distribution	$ 730,000	$ 808,000	$ 893,800	$ 988,180	$ 1,091,998
Cost Margins:					
Cost of Sales	25.0%	25.0%	25.0%	25.0%	25.0%
Labor Expense	30.0%	30.0%	30.0%	30.0%	30.0%
Operating Expense	25.0%	25.0%	25.0%	25.0%	25.0%
Profit Margins:					
Gross Profit	75.0%	75.0%	75.0%	75.0%	75.0%
Pretax Income	20.0%	20.0%	20.0%	20.0%	20.0%
Net Income	13.0%	13.0%	13.0%	13.0%	13.0%
Unit Statistics:					
Square Footage	5,000	5,000	5,000	5,000	5,000
Seats	150	150	150	150	150
Check Average	$ 40	$ 40	$ 40	$ 40	$ 40

FIGURE 24.3 Analysis of Entrepreneur B's Projected Income Statements

ENTREPRENEUR B—XYZ RESTAURANT
ANALYSIS OF PROJECTED INCOME STATEMENTS
FOR THE YEARS ENDING . . .

	Year 1	Year 2	Year 3	Year 4	Year 5
Sales per Year	$6,000,000	$6,600,000	$7,260,000	$7,986,000	$8,784,600
Sales per Week	$ 115,385	$ 126,923	$ 139,615	$ 153,577	$ 168,935
Sales per Day	$ 16,484	$ 18,132	$ 19,945	$ 21,940	$ 24,134
Guests per Day	659	725	798	878	965
Table-Turns	6.6	7.3	8.0	8.8	9.7
Sales per Square Foot	$ 1,200	$ 1,320	$ 1,452	$ 1,597	$ 1,757

assume that each table-turn occurs every one hour (which would be fast for a $40 check average) and peak hours are 12:00 PM to 2:00 PM and 7:00 PM to 9:00 PM, then we realize that the projected table-turns are, for all intents and purposes, unattainable. (This requires 100 percent occupancy with one-hour table-turns during peak hours seven days a week and an additional 2.5 turns per day during non-peak hours.) The investors' conclusion should be that the projections are utterly unrealistic and they should pass on the opportunity. Further, Entrepreneur B is likely to run an extremely high payroll relative to revenue. She will staff the company to generate $6 million in sales, which we have determined is all but impossible.

In examining Entrepreneur A's projections in Figure 24.4, we find that he projects $700 per square foot in sales for his restaurant in Year 1 and $851 per square foot in sales in Year 5. Year 1's projections per square foot are 75 percent greater than the industry average. It is important to note that if your projections are much less, it is probably not worth launching the project. No one will invest in an independent restaurant that intends to equal the national chain average.

FIGURE 24.4 Analysis of Entrepreneur A's Projected Income Statements

ENTREPRENEUR A—XYZ RESTAURANT
ANALYSIS OF PROJECTED INCOME STATEMENTS
FOR THE YEARS ENDING . . .

	Year 1	Year 2	Year 3	Year 4	Year 5
Sales per Year	$3,500,000	$3,675,000	$3,858,750	$4,051,688	$4,254,272
Sales per Week	$ 67,308	$ 70,673	$ 74,207	$ 77,917	$ 01,013
Sales per Day	$ 9,615	$ 10,096	$ 10,601	$ 11,131	$ 11,688
Guests per Day	240	252	265	278	292
Table-Turns	1.6	1.7	1.8	1.9	1.9
Sales per Square Foot	$ 700	$ 735	$ 772	$ 810	$ 851

Entrepreneur A's table-turns are much more reasonable than are Entrepreneur B's as well. Entrepreneur A projects his restaurant will have 1.6 table-turns per night in Year 1 and 1.9 table-turns per night in Year 5. I believe that Entrepreneur A's projections are more believable than are Entrepreneur B's. Unfortunately, in many instances, Entrepreneur B's project will be funded and Entrepreneur A's project will not.

The answer to this problem is to not inflate your projections. Projections should represent what you believe is the expected financial position, results of operations, and changes in financial position (cash flows) for your project for the projected period. Recognize that there will be differences between the projection and the actual results, because events and circumstances frequently don't occur as expected, and those differences may be material. Your projections should always be your best guess, and you should be able to support those projects with competitive analyses and historical financials.

An investment group interested in Entrepreneur B's project brings many challenges to the entrepreneur-investor relationship.

If the group's expectations are too badly skewed, Entrepreneur B will find that even if she duplicates the success of The Cheesecake Factory, she will be considered just another restaurant entrepreneur who overpromises and underdelivers.

25

VOTING RIGHTS

Identify clearly who has the power.

No matter how long and complex, all operating agreements come down to a few key terms. For your investors, these key terms are *ownership percentage* and *voting rights*. As I have previously described, ownership percentage is generally in the forefront of the entrepreneur-investor relationship initially. Voting rights outline how much control your investors will have in the company, a matter generally not contentious unless operations materially underperform relative to expectations.

In reality, voting rights take two forms: those printed in the shareholder's agreement and those in practice. For example, a sole, high-net-worth investor may have as much say in a company's business decisions as he or she wants, irrespective of the operating agreement. And you may have very little power. Often, whoever has the deepest pockets wins voting disputes in small businesses. The 800-pound gorilla sits wherever it wants.

As the entrepreneur, you should have operational control. In most cases, investors expect, and may even insist, on this. After all, the investment was based on your vision and your promise to create that vision. You must be given the authority to make the necessary operational decisions. However, investors become concerned if you don't hit your numbers. You will be measured by results, and the results appear on your financial statements. I have had managers who were operating an underperforming asset try to explain to me that "a lot of the business isn't shown on the financial statements." This is nonsense. I would expect a company with a strong culture to have lower employee turnover. And lower employee turnover should result in lower human resources expense and training cost. The entire business is represented in the financial statements. I understand that projections often differ materially from actual results, but the entrepreneur is charged with creating shareholder wealth and nothing else.

Investors typically recognize that injecting their operational views is counterproductive, creating bureaucracy where nimbleness is needed for survival. However, investors generally want a vote on key nonoperational matters, such as a sale of the asset, a bankruptcy decision, debt acquisition, corporate guarantees, and key management compensation. Ideally, all decisions on these matters should be mutual. I don't believe in drawing lines between limited partners and general partners; all partners have insight, and all partners generally have a great deal at stake.

ASSET SALE

In considering the sale of a restaurant for a negative return, investors believe they are entitled to a vote. I agree, provided the entrepreneur has not signed a noncompete contract or any clause that requires the consent of the investors for the entrepreneur to remove himself or herself from the business. If the entrepreneur has signed a noncompete or is not capable of exiting the business without the consent of the majority, the entrepreneur is in checkmate and can't continue to operate a failing business but yet can't exit. Again, an investment group often has no incentive to accept a deal that gives it a return less than expectations; therefore, the entrepreneur must continue to operate the business regardless of the personal consequences.

When a business faces challenges and is losing money, management salaries are often decreased to stop the hemorrhaging. The question for the entrepreneur becomes: How long should the entrepreneur operate a failing business before the investment group concedes to selling at a loss? If the business is underperforming but not requiring capital calls, investors have little incentive to sell.

The commonly held belief is that an entrepreneur sold investors on buying a percentage of the business; therefore, the entrepreneur should work to return the capital. I believe this is true. However, when is a business no longer a viable investment? Individual investors will keep the investment on their balance sheet and not write down the value until the investment is sold. Whether keeping their heads in the sand or not, investors are not recognizing the true value of the asset. All the while, the entrepreneur must work for reduced pay with no bonus or maybe work even for free. The agreements need to be crafted so the entrepreneur can move on and the investors can find new management.

BANKRUPTCY

In the case of a decision to file for bankruptcy, the investors want to make their own determination of whether bankruptcy is the optimal course of action. Investors want a vote to file for either liquidation or restructuring. Bankruptcy issues are very complex, but one point in particular is important to understand: Payroll and tax issues aren't recognized in bankruptcy. Investors, depending on their role in the company, may be liable along with the entrepreneur for the full amount of tax and payroll debt. Further, all parties who have had an influence in operations, whether an investor or a manager, may be both jointly and severally liable for the company's debts.

DEBT ACQUISITION

Investors will also demand a vote on the matter of additional corporate debts and/or guarantees. Investors have the right to understand the source and use of all capital. Payments of principal and interest affect free cash flow and therefore the investors' returns. The addition of an assistant manager will also negatively affect distributable cash, but this staffing matter is both operational and controllable whereas debt payments are not. In short, the company is bound to pay the debt where the assistant manager can be let go.

CORPORATE GUARANTEES

Guarantees do not affect operating capital, but they do have an effect on the proceeds from an exit. If the entrepreneur binds the company to a five-year lease and has the opportunity to sell the unit, the company will have to pay the remainder of the lease obligation from the proceeds. Guarantees limit the flexibility of the company, so investors are reasonable in requesting a voice in the decision.

MANAGEMENT COMPENSATION

Another topic of investor concern is management raises. In independent restaurants, very little need exists for management raises. A well-crafted deal has the incentives of all the parties aligned and tied to performance. The entrepreneur and key management should share in cash flow distributions. Further, the entrepreneur should own a percentage of the capital. By participating in cash flow, those in management, as owners, have the luxury of determining their own destiny. If the entrepreneur wants a raise, then he or she should drive the top line and cut costs to get the raise in the form of greater cash flow.

26

NONCASH LIABILITIES

All liabilities have a claim against the assets.

Your deal is complete. You have acquired funding, and you have executed the operating agreement. Your liabilities have just begun. Assume you retain 25 percent of the equity, based on your track record and business plan. Now it's time to execute the lease. If your ownership negotiations were not predicated on a guarantee (including a good-guy clause), you should not be the sole underwriter of the lease. You have no more obligation than do any of the partners to sign a personal guarantee. Liability requires compensation.

AN EXAMPLE

A 5,000-square-foot casual-dining restaurant could spend more than $30,000 on a good point-of-sale computer (POS). You may determine that leasing is an attractive option, but it is all but impossible to lease a POS without providing a personal guarantee.

Assume an investment of $500,000 for a new restaurant project is structured as a limited liability company. Entrepreneur A negotiated a salary of $40,000 a year plus 25 percent ownership offering significant bonus potential. Assume that Entrepreneur A guaranteed a $10,000 per month, five-year lease on the building and also guaranteed a POS lease at $1,000 per month for five years.

The business opens to great crowds. Traffic exceeds expectations. At the end of the first year, Entrepreneur A distributes $100,000 to the investment group. At the beginning of Year 2, a similar restaurant opens across the street. Sales decline 20 percent. Next, the city elects to repair the street out front. The repair work diverts traffic and sales decline a further 25 percent. In Year 2, sales have declined 40 percent over Year 1, and Entrepreneur A accepts one-half his salary until business rebounds. Cash flow remains tight; in Year 3, the investors elect to close the business to avoid a capital call.

The investors are unhappy with their investment results, and many blame Entrepreneur A. After the business is closed, the assets, with the exception of the POS, are sold to pay the employees, taxes, and purveyors. So far, neither rent on the building nor the POS have been paid in Year 3. Assume asset sales net $50,000 and investors write off the remaining losses. Therefore, investors in the 39 percent tax bracket will collectively lose $210,000 on the investment. Entrepreneur A, however, faces a liability of $396,000— 36 months of rent and POS payments.

Now why would Entrepreneur A run the company in Year 2 for $20,000 and accept $396,000 of liability for an ownership percentage of 25 percent? It happens all the time as the result of false trust and poor planning. When an investment goes bad, there are no friends. And don't expect your partners to "do the right thing." My suggestion is to plan correctly, meaning that you identify all liabilities before executing any agreements, get everything in writing, and don't guarantee anything. Always behave ethically and bind all partners in an agreement that requires them to act ethically, because the investors will most likely blame the entrepreneur for any negative result.

27

EXITING THE BUSINESS

Exiting at a premium is the ultimate goal.

Most entrepreneurs are so certain that their business will set the new standard for the industry that they don't plan for anything short of a wild success. Businesses are generally simple to form and easy to launch but difficult to wind down. In light of the restaurant industry's 95 percent failure rate, you should generate an exit strategy in tandem with development of the concept. The exit may be the most significant strategy the entrepreneur ever develops.

Entrepreneurs who are crafting their first deal and need investors most likely need a paycheck as well. What happens if a business is not successful? How financially exposed is the entrepreneur? How long can the entrepreneur go without taking a salary? How many businesses does the entrepreneur have that generate cash flow?

My first restaurant deal was a disaster. It was the Atlantic Pearl in Boulder, Colorado. The business was separated into two divisions—the bar and the restaurant. The bar, under the management of my partner, Jonathan Broadhurst, was successful. It was full nearly every night. The restaurant had wonderful food reviews but very few customers. For every penny we made in the bar, we lost two in the restaurant. Within the year, the writing was on the wall—the business plan, as written, was a failure. With the hindsight of experience, we should have closed the restaurant and used all of our assets to grow the bar business.

However, I was not prepared for the restaurant's low volume. Without an exit strategy, I spent the last months of the Atlantic Pearl's existence working without a salary. I was forced into an unfortunately common entrepreneurial conundrum—whether to pay the mortgage on my home or buy product for the business. I used personal money to buy chickens to keep the business alive because I didn't know what else to do. The restaurant was more than my job; it was my responsibility and more than a little bit of my identity. Finally, we recognized that a sale was our only option and we walked away. For me, the Atlantic Pearl was traumatic but an indispensable learning experience. Without this failure, I would never have enrolled in business school to seek an MBA.

Exit decisions are fairly simple when a business is a disaster. Decisions become difficult when the business is operating near breakeven. The business may be operating but at what cost? The entrepreneur, most likely, will have to accept a pay decrease. Management pay reductions are not at all unusual in start-ups. The entrepreneur generally negotiates a small salary with bonus potential and ownership in the business. Before the business opens and before the agreements signed, a contingency plan must be developed. I believe the best approach is to conduct a "what if" exercise. For instance:

- **What if the business is wildly successful?** Are you the right manager to operate a stable and successful business, or are you best suited to operate at start-up or in a crisis?
- **What if the business is marginally successful?** Do you want to spend years of your life operating a business that has not

met your financial expectations? Sometimes changing your expectations is easier than changing your business.

- **What if the business operates below breakeven?** Can you sustain long periods with a reduced salary or no salary at all? How will you react when you realize that your plans of building an empire are put on hold to operate a failing business?
- **What if the business is a dog?** Are you capable of recognizing a failed business before your investors, purveyors, or the Internal Revenue Service does? Can you withstand the pressure of not knowing where your next paycheck will come from?
- **What if there is an opportunity to sell the business at a favorable multiple?** Do you view this business as your creation, your baby? Will you be willing to sell it?

In drafting an exit strategy, consider a scenario in which you are successful but the business faces challenges. Be very clear how you intend to move forward in each scenario. The key question that must be asked under any projected condition is where the value is. For example, although the asset may be underperforming, the lease may have value if you negotiated a favorable assignable clause. In each instance, the entrepreneur must be fearlessly honest and identify and communicate the strategy to the investment group. If the business operates below breakeven and you are required to accept a portion of your agreed-on salary, what will you do? If you intend to walk away, the investors have a right to know prior to executing contracts. You may have to walk away for such an honorable reason as the need to provide for your family; the result, however, will be negative for the investors. You can't ask investors to fund your deal with the knowledge that if the deal performs at, or better than, what is projected, you are the right person for the job, but if the deal faces challenges, you will abort.

Perversely, a successful business can be as troubling as a failing business. Very few presidents/CEOs can operate businesses in all business cycles. For example, entrepreneurs are generally great problem solvers; and they think quickly on their feet. However, daily problems arise when a business stabilizes and will challenge entrepreneurs with the transition from reactionary problem solving to strategic problem solving. Exiting a business requires foresight, and your remuneration depends critically on exiting properly. If nothing else, we have established that projections often differ materially from actual results. Therefore, consider the exit plan a critical component of your business plan.

28

STRUCTURING THE DEAL

All incentives must be aligned.

How much do I offer my investors? I get this question a lot. I find that most restaurant entrepreneurs don't understand the relationship between invested capital, cash flow, and ownership percentage. Private equity investors seek IRRs greater than those available in the public markets. A private restaurant investor demands a risk premium, which is warranted given that the investment is most often illiquid and carries systematic risk as well as tremendous unsystematic risk.

No standard structure exists for private investment deals. Each investor evaluates the risk and sets an ownership percentage according to his or her analysis. The level of comfort derives from the management team, the concept, and the market. Here are a few points to keep in mind when arranging the deal:

- Your percentage of ownership will be directly related to your track record, the amount of capital you have at risk, and the pool of willing investors. A restaurateur like Steven Starr can structure a deal that returns investors' money plus a slight return on capital. He has a strong negotiating position because he has been successful, and most investors believe that his new venture will succeed.

- Don't view your first deal as your last deal. You won't be able to structure an acceptable deal if you aren't willing to build a track record.
- Don't compare your deals to industry stars. I often hear what a Todd English or Roy Yamaguchi deal looks like. If you aren't a proven star, their deals are not relevant. In simple terms: Do what they did and you can get what they got.
- Losing a bad deal is better than winning it. Once the operating agreement has been signed, you have to live with the deal. Therefore, understand all of your liabilities before structuring the agreement.
- Treat your investors fairly and respectfully. Being the steward of investors' capital is an honor and a tremendous responsibility.
- Your job is to create shareholder wealth, not a better life. Your personal goals are secondary to your fiduciary responsibilities.
- Your investors are your partners. Your career will be difficult if you have to create a new shareholder group for each project. Your current investors are your best source of capital. If current investors aren't interested, why would other investors be?
- Private equity funds, professional investors, and venture capital groups expect approximately 80 percent ownership for 100 percent of the capital.
- Individual investors expect at least 50 percent of your company and will want to recover 100 percent of their capital plus interest before you, the entrepreneur, participate in cash flow.

In Chapter 17, we learned the basics of financial modeling for a restaurant enterprise. Now we complete the picture with a discussion of the entrepreneur's share of the business.

You can negotiate a straight salary or a percentage of sales. I believe that a small percentage of sales is more appropriate because it provides an incentive to drive the top line. I have projected the entrepreneur's compensation as 2.5 percent of sales, which is booked as General and Administrative Expense. Figure 28.1 is our monthly income statement for XYZ Restaurant. Figure 28.2 is XYZ Restaurant's annual income statement for five years. In Year 2 through Year 5, I assume that sales will grow at a rate of 5 percent and Labor Cost will grow at a rate of 3 percent.

I assumed that the company is a tax-holding entity, so investors pay taxes on the pretax income. Further, I have assumed that the investors pay taxes at a 39 percent marginal rate—the highest tax bracket. Now we can determine cash flow available for distribution (see Figure 28.3).

I assume the investors contributed $800,000 and the entrepreneur receives a bonus of 10 percent of all cash flow above $200,000. The $200,000 hurdle was selected to give the investors a 25 percent return on equity before the entrepreneur received a bonus.

Figure 28.4 illustrates inflows and outflows as well as the percentage of cash flow required for the investors to achieve a 25 percent IRR. In our example, investors need to own 68 percent of the restaurant to achieve this desired return. Therefore, the entrepreneur receives the remaining 32 percent. You see that the ownership percentage is determined by cash flow. Had the entrepreneur persuaded investors that the company was more profitable or less risky, the entrepreneur's ownership percentage would be higher. Remember that the percentage of ownership applies only to cash flow distribution. Voting rights are determined separately in corporate agreements. Figure 28.5 illustrates the entrepreneur's entire compensation package.

Many ways are available to structure a deal. A deal with a wealthy relative will be considerably different from a deal with a professional investor. A deal structured before you have a track record will differ considerably from a deal structured after you have operated a company that has created shareholder wealth.

FIGURE 28.1 Projected Monthly Income Statements

XYZ RESTAURANT
INCOME STATEMENTS FOR THE MONTHS ENDING . . .

	July	August	September	October	November	December	January
Revenue:							
Food	$ 113,440	$ 167,750	$ 250,100	$ 274,500	$ 250,100	$ 305,000	$ 228,750
Beverage	73,360	107,250	159,900	175,500	159,900	195,000	146,250
Total Revenue	186,800	275,000	410,000	450,000	410,000	500,000	375,000
Cost of Sales:							
Food	37,435	55,358	82,533	90,585	82,533	100,650	75,488
Beverage	18,340	26,813	39,975	43,875	39,975	48,750	36,563
Total Cost of Sales	55,775	82,170	122,508	134,460	122,508	149,400	112,050
Gross Profit	131,025	192,830	287,492	315,540	287,492	350,600	262,950
Labor Cost:							
Payroll	94,116	94,116	94,116	94,116	94,116	94,116	94,116
Payroll Tax	20,706	20,706	20,706	20,706	20,706	20,706	20,706
Total Labor Cost	114,822	114,822	114,822	114,822	114,822	114,822	114,822
Operating Expenses	50,436	74,250	110,700	121,500	110,700	135,000	101,250
General and Administrative Expense	4,670	6,875	10,250	11,250	10,250	12,500	9,375
Pretax Income	(38,903)	(3,117)	51,720	67,968	51,720	88,278	37,503
Income Tax	na	na	na	na	na	na	na
Net Income	$ (38,903)	$ (3,117)	$ 51,720	$ 67,968	$ 51,720	$ 88,278	$ 37,503

	February	March	April	May	June	Year End
Revenue:						
Food	$ 213,500	$ 244,000	$ 244,000	$ 256,200	$ 244,000	$2,791,340
Beverage	136,500	156,000	156,000	163,800	156,000	1,785,460
Total Revenue	350,000	400,000	400,000	420,000	400,000	4,576,800
Cost of Sales:						
Food	70,455	80,520	80,520	84,546	80,520	921,142
Beverage	34,125	39,000	39,000	40,950	39,000	446,365
Total Cost of Sales	104,580	119,520	119,520	125,496	119,520	1,367,507
Gross Profit	245,420	280,480	280,480	294,504	280,480	3,209,293
Labor Cost:						
Payroll	94,116	94,116	94,116	94,116	94,116	1,129,392
Payroll Tax	20,706	20,706	20,706	20,706	20,706	248,466
Total Labor Cost	114,822	114,822	114,822	114,822	114,822	1,377,858
Operating Expenses	94,500	108,000	108,000	113,400	108,000	1,235,736
General and Administrative Expense	8,750	10,000	10,000	10,500	10,000	114,420
Pretax Income	27,348	47,658	47,658	55,782	47,658	481,279
Income Tax	na	na	na	na	na	(187,699)
Net Income	$ 27,348	$ 47,658	$ 47,658	$ 55,782	$ 47,658	$ 293,580

FIGURE 28.2 Projected Annual Income Statements

XYZ RESTAURANT
INCOME STATEMENTS
FOR THE YEARS ENDING . . .

	Year 1	Year 2	Year 3	Year 4	Year 5
Revenue:					
Food	$2,791,340	$2,930,907	$3,077,452	$3,231,325	$3,392,891
Beverage	1,785,460	1,874,733	1,968,470	2,066,893	2,170,238
Total Revenue	4,576,800	4,805,640	5,045,922	5,298,218	5,563,129
Cost of Sales:					
Food	921,142	967,199	1,015,559	1,066,337	1,119,654
Beverage	446,365	468,683	492,117	516,723	542,559
Total Cost of Sales	1,367,507	1,435,883	1,507,677	1,583,061	1,662,214
Gross Profit	3,209,293	3,369,757	3,538,245	3,715,158	3,900,915
Labor Cost:					
Payroll	1,129,392	1,163,274	1,198,172	1,234,117	1,271,141
Payroll Tax	248,466	255,920	263,598	271,506	279,651
Total Labor Cost	1,377,858	1,419,194	1,461,770	1,505,623	1,550,792
Operating Expenses	1,235,736	1,297,523	1,362,399	1,430,519	1,502,045
General and Administrative Expense	114,420	120,141	126,148	132,455	139,078
Pretax Income	481,279	653,041	714,077	779,016	848,079
Income Tax	(187,699)	(254,686)	(278,490)	(303,816)	(330,751)
Net Income	$ 293,580	$ 398,355	$ 435,587	$ 475,200	$ 517,328

FIGURE 28.3 Projected Simple Cash Flow Statements

XYZ RESTAURANT
SIMPLE CASH FLOW STATEMENTS FOR THE YEARS ENDING . . .

	Year 1	Year 2	Year 3	Year 4	Year 5
Net Income	$293,580	$398,355	$435,587	$475,200	$517,328
Entrepreneur's Bonus	(9,358)	(19,835)	(23,559)	(27,520)	(31,733)
Capital Expenditures	—	(50,000)	(50,000)	(50,000)	(50,000)
Free Cash Flow	$284,222	$328,519	$362,028	$397,680	$435,595

FIGURE 28.4 Internal-Rate-of-Return Analysis

XYZ RESTAURANT
IRR ANALYSIS FOR THE YEARS ENDING . . .

	Year 0	Year 1	Year 2	Year 3	Year 4	Year 5
Investment	$ 800,000	$ —	$ —	$ —	$ —	$ —
Free Cash Flow	—	284,222	328,519	362,028	397,680	435,595
Investors' Payback	—	284,222	328,519	187,259		
Free Cash Flow after Investors' Payback	—	—	—	174,769	397,680	435,595
Additional Cash Flow for Required IRR	—	—	—	118,843	270,422	296,205
Total Investor Cash Flow Distributions	$(800,000)	$ 284,222	$ 328,519	$ 306,102	$ 270,422	$ 296,205
Investor IRR	25%					

FIGURE 28.5 Entrepreneur's Compensation

	Year 1	Year 2	Year 3	Year 4	Year 5
XYZ RESTAURANT					
TOTAL DISTRIBUTIONS TO THE ENTREPRENEUR					
FOR THE YEARS ENDING . . .					
Entrepreneur's Distributions					
Management Fee	$114,420	$120,141	$126,148	$132,455	$139,078
Bonus	9,358	19,835	23,559	27,520	31,733
Cash Flow Distributions	–	–	55,926	127,257	139,391
Total Entrepreneur Compensation	$123,778	$139,976	$205,633	$287,233	$310,202

The deal crafted in my example is one that protects the investors in that their capital is repaid before any bonus is paid to the entrepreneur. The entrepreneur, after returning the risk capital, is compensated with a significant ownership stake and cash flow participation.

Most entrepreneurs I have met believe that investors fund a project and the entrepreneur does the work. Consider money as work. In most every instance other than inherited wealth, investors' capital represents work by those investors. In the case of inherited wealth, some family member had to work for the money being invested in the entrepreneur's deal. Investors want to know that the entrepreneur respects their capital and that the entrepreneur will make money pari passu with the investors. Investors become concerned if an entrepreneur has the opportunity to generate a handsome return on his or her efforts before, or at the expense of, the investors. All incentives must be aligned.

In meetings with prospective investors, an entrepreneur must clearly outline what he or she is projected to make in salary, bonus, and distributions and what the investors are projected to make in the deal. Further, if there are incentives tied to sales that would allow the entrepreneur to benefit to the detriment of the investors' returns, the entrepreneur must identify those scenarios. A successful deal requires full transparency. Interestingly, the clearer the financial picture and the more disclosure the entrepreneur offers, the more likely the investors will be interested in the deal. It is not the entrepreneur's position to sell the deal. All benefits should certainly be identified, but the entrepreneur must simply report the facts and provide all information necessary for investors to make an educated investment decision.

It is better for the entrepreneur to identify the risks for investors than for investors to identify the risks for the entrepreneur. For example, as an investor reviews the project statement of profit and loss, the entrepreneur should outline the reasons that the business will not meet its projections as well as exceed its projections. A restaurant's sales are the result of traffic and check average. What are the reasons traffic may be less than projected? In the event that traffic is below expectations, what will the entrepreneur's course of action be? How would check average be affected by a downturn in the economy? Identifying the risks to investors shows that the entrepreneur understands the position of the investors. In capital raising, the entrepreneur must be perceived as an educated industry expert and not a salesperson.

WELCOME TO THE WORLD'S GREATEST INDUSTRY

29

READING THE TEA LEAVES

Good data are the key to good decisions.

Today's restaurant entrepreneurs act as presidents of small companies. They require timely data allowing them to make swift, educated decisions. Daily analysis of restaurant metrics allows the entrepreneurs to determine precisely what the market is saying. Analysis in the restaurant industry should be a daily event. I have developed a few reports that assist in the management of the business. The reports provide a level of detail whereby I can quickly assess the business and any trends that are developing. This chapter is intended to be an overview; the material covered could be an entirely separate book.

REPORTS

Figure 29.1 is a quick report that restaurateurs should view each morning. The report was designed for a dinner-only restaurant that generates additional sales with its bar. Total net sales, check average, and traffic are the critical data points in absolute

FIGURE 29.1 Daily Report

	XYZ RESTAURANT DAILY REPORT			
	Day 1		**Day 2**	
Gross Food Sales	$	–	$	–
Gross Beverage Sales:				
Beer		–		–
Wine		–		–
Liquor		–		–
Nonalcoholic		–		–
Total Gross Liquor Sales		–		–
Private Parties		–		–
Total Gross Sales		–		–
Total Comps		–		–
Food Comps		–		–
Food Comps @ 33%		–		–
Beverage Comps		–		–
Beverage Cost @ 25%		–		–
Total Comps		–		–
Sales Tax:				
Sales Tax Included		–		–
Sales Tax Extra		–		–
Total Sales Tax		–		–
Net Food Sales		–		–
Net Beverage Sales		–		–
Total Net Sales		–		–
Food and Beverage		–		–
Customers—Traffic		–		–
Average Check per Customer		–		–
Dining Room		–		–
Customers—Traffic		–		–
Average Check per Customer		–		–
Bar		–		–
Customers—Traffic		–		–
Average Check per Customer		–		–

dollars as well as in trends. Simply studying total net sales can be misleading; they are generated by check average times traffic. Figure 29.2 illustrates a restaurant's traffic and check average. Examining the trend of the components, a restaurateur will uncover a troubling fact. Total net sales may be trending positive and meeting expectations at the same time that traffic is declining and check average increasing. It appears that fewer consumers are patronizing the business, and those who do are spending more money. Ideally, a restaurant can maintain a consistent check average and increase traffic. A $12 casual-dining check average is quickly trending to an upper-end casual-dining check average without increasing the value to the guests. The guests who spend the money, though, may be finding value. This analysis leads to an evaluation of what the guests value.

I find that key labor and venue utilization metrics help manage the business (see Figure 29.3). Labor metrics assist in trend analysis. Figure 29.3 charts the labor metrics by the week.

FIGURE 29.2 Trend Analysis: Check Average and Traffic

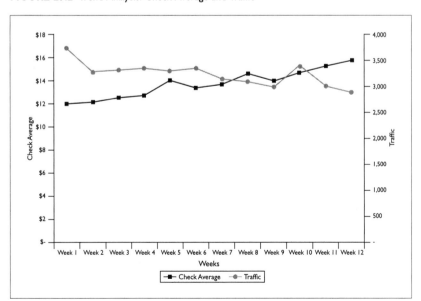

FIGURE 29.3 Key Metric Analysis

	Week 1	Week 2	Week 3	Week 4
XYZ RESTAURANT **KEY METRIC REPORT**				
Labor Metrics:				
Kitchen controllable hours to food sales	1.7	1.8	1.9	2.3
Front of the house controllable hours to total sales	2.2	2.1	2.1	2.0
Bar controllable hours to bar sales	1.9	2.9	1.7	3.7
Venue Utilization:				
Lunch sales	$16,500	$14,000	$17,050	$18,300
Lunch table-turn times (in minutes)	45	60	40	32
Dinner sales	$32,000	$28,400	$30,300	$26,050
Dinner table-turn times (in minutes)	90	75	85	70

An examination of Figure 29.4 shows that the kitchen is becoming less efficient, the front of the house is becoming more efficient, and the bar is suffering from either erratic sales or the bar manager's need for help in scheduling.

Figure 29.5 shows what appears to be an inverse relationship between table-turns times and lunch sales. After collecting more data points, the restaurateur may attempt to streamline the lunch menu to reduce the minutes per table-turn and possibly increase lunch sales.

Figure 29.6 shows a direct correlation between dinner sales and table-turn times. Specifically, the longer the average table-turn time, the higher the dinner sales. After collecting more data points the restaurateur may attempt to offer additional services during the dinner hour—for example, after-dinner drinks or elaborate desserts.

FIGURE 29.4 Labor Metric Analysis

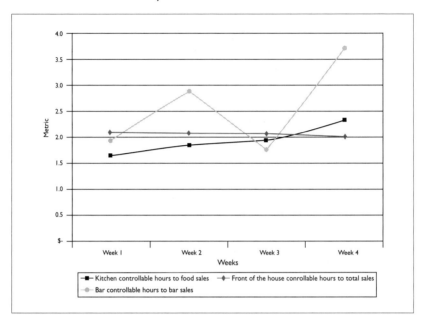

FIGURE 29.5 Lunch Venue Utilization Analysis

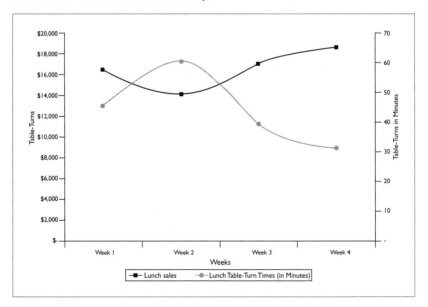

FIGURE 29.6 Dinner Venue Utilization Analysis

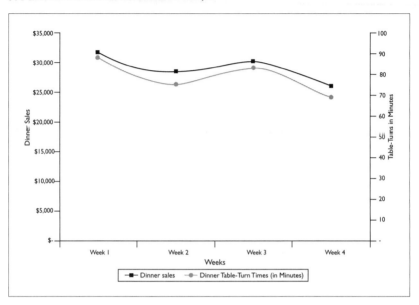

MENU AUDIT

The final report that I suggest restaurateurs create is the menu audit, which shows which menu items make the greatest contribution. The menu audit factors in sales, food cost, and labor cost. To begin, separate your menu by category—for example, appetizers, entrées, side orders, and desserts. Next, gather from your POS system the number of items sold over the past three months by category. Ask your kitchen manager or chef to provide the food cost percentage per menu item and estimate the labor cost per menu item. The lowest labor percentage should be 10 percent and the highest labor percentage 50 percent. Now, enter data into the Menu Audit Worksheet. Figure 29.7 is an example from an upper-end restaurant.

Figure 29.8 ranks the appetizers for contribution after food cost. The sweetbread Napoleon appears to be the most profitable item. Figure 29.9 ranks the sample of appetizers after labor cost

FIGURE 29.7 Menu Audit Worksheet

APPETIZERS	# SOLD PER NIGHT	# SOLD PER QUARTER	PRICE	FOOD COST	CONTRIBUTION AFTER FOOD COST	LABOR COST	CONTRIBUTION BY ITEM	CONTRIBUTION BY QUARTER
Caesar Salad	20	1,800	$ 8	20%	$ 6.40	25%	$4.40	$7,920
French Onion Soup	18	1,620	8	16%	6.72	30%	4.32	6,998
Tomato Salad	12	1,080	9	18%	7.38	20%	5.58	6,026
Foie Gras	8	720	14	30%	9.80	20%	7.00	5,040
Crab Cakes	12	1,080	12	25%	9.00	40%	4.20	4,536
Sweetbread Napoleon	4	360	14	25%	10.50	40%	4.90	1,764
Mixed Green Salad	14	1,260	6	15%	5.10	20%	3.90	4,914

FIGURE 29.8 Appetizers Contribution after Food Cost

APPETIZERS	CONTRIBUTION AFTER FOOD COST
Sweetbread Napoleon	$10.50
Foie Gras	9.80
Crab Cakes	9.00
Tomato Salad	7.38
French Onion Soup	6.72
Caesar Salad	6.40
Mixed Green Salad	5.10

FIGURE 29.9 Appetizers Contribution after Labor Cost

APPETIZERS	CONTRIBUTION BY ITEM
Foie Gras	$7.00
Tomato Salad	5.58
Sweetbread Napoleon	4.90
Caesar Salad	4.40
French Onion Soup	4.32
Crab Cakes	4.20
Mixed Green Salad	3.90

has been accounted for. Contribution after labor cost suggests that the foie gras is the most profitable item. Figure 29.10 ranks the sample appetizers by operating margin and weighting of sales. In examining Figure 29.11, we see the benefit of the menu audit. When we simply look at food cost, the sweetbread Napoleon appears to be the best contributor to operating income. After a full

FIGURE 29.10 Appetizers Sorted by Operating Margin, Weighted by Sales

APPETIZERS	CONTRIBUTION BY QUARTER
Caesar Salad	$7,920
French Onion Soup	6,998
Tomato Salad	6,026
Foie Gras	5,040
Mixed Green Salad	4,914
Crab Cakes	4,536
Sweetbread Napoleon	1,764

FIGURE 29.11 Summary Results of the Menu Audit

APPETIZERS	CONTRIBUTION AFTER FOOD COST
Sweetbread Napoleon	$10.50
Foie Gras	9.80
Crab Cakes	9.00
Tomato Salad	7.38
French Onion Soup	6.72
Caesar Salad	6.40
Mixed Green Salad	5.10

APPETIZERS	CONTRIBUTION BY ITEM
Foie Gras	$7.00
Tomato Salad	5.58
Sweetbread Napoleon	4.90
Caesar Salad	4.40
French Onion Soup	4.32
Crab Cakes	4.20
Mixed Green Salad	3.90

APPETIZERS	CONTRIBUTION BY QUARTER
Caesar Salad	$7,920
French Onion Soup	6,998
Tomato Salad	6,026
Foie Gras	5,040
Mixed Green Salad	4,914
Crab Cakes	4,536
Sweetbread Napoleon	1,764

examination, however, the sweetbread Napoleon may have to be removed from the menu. It appears to use an inordinate amount of kitchen labor relative to its contribution to operating income. Figure 29.11 summarizes the menu audit results.

30

A DAY IN A LIFE

Congratulations, you are now a businessperson.

The restaurant industry combines art and science perfectly. A restaurateur's day is spent focusing on the details that make a customer's experience memorable as well as analyzing guests' data, meeting with ad agencies, developing marketing strategies, researching new products, creating joint ventures, and motivating the staff. The industry comprises people from all walks of life. The life can be very appealing, very glamorous. Each day is a new event—new guests, new opportunities.

A day in the life of a restaurateur can be as invigorating as it is exhausting. It is true that restaurant employees work a great many hours, but as in every other industry I know of, success is predicated on hard work.

The day begins early with an examination of the prior day's results. The restaurateur quickly analyzes the data. The key questions are these:

- How did we do yesterday relative to the budget?
- How did we do yesterday relative to the same day last week?

- What is the week-over-week trend from last year?
- Was our sales mix optimal, or did we sell too much food relative to high-margin beverages?

Next, a quick call to the bookkeeper to request a labor report showing controllable labor for lunch service relative to lunch sales and controllable labor for dinner service relative to dinner sales. The bookkeeper's guess is that lunch sales may be contributing too little to justify the labor expense under the current format. More in-depth analysis has to wait until after the meeting with the public relations firm.

The public relations firm presents its concept for the upcoming quarter. The firm believes that more work with charities will raise the profile of the business and offers a list of upcoming charitable events. The restaurant can supply food and meals for auction with minimal cost but gaining immense exposure. When confronted with last month's lack of PR output, the public relations firm gives the usual long list of excuses—the weather, too many openings, overexposure, and so on. Finally, the representatives of the PR firm ask for their check because they have to meet another client. As they leave, the restaurateur ponders why he didn't go into a business based on retainers rather than results.

It is now midmorning, and the meeting with the event planner is set to begin. For the third consecutive month, the event planner did not meet projections. The discussion begins with the event planner's outlining capital improvements needed to improve event sales. Further, the event planner outlines $50,000 of advertising that she believes will boost sales. The restaurateur decides that a new event planner must be hired because this gal has used the same excuses before. The meeting is cut short.

Time for one last meeting with the bookkeeper before lunch service. After analyzing the bookkeeper's lunch-versus-dinner labor report, the restaurateur realizes his instincts were correct: Lunch labor is too high relative to lunch sales. Overall labor expense is in line as a percentage of total revenue, so it would be easy to determine, without the bookkeeper's in-depth analysis, that no adjustments to labor are necessary. Next, the restaurateur asks the office manager for the results of the past three weeks' lunch customer feedback reports. (Each day the wait staff documents guests comments and the office manager keys the comments into a report form). The restaurateur will attempt to review the guests' comments during his daily lunch, where he observes the dining room and the guests' experience.

During his lunch, the restaurateur recognizes that the guest feedback is remarkably consistent. First, the time it takes for lunch is too long, and, second, the menu needs more casual items. The restaurateur believes that he has the answer to solve the lunch problem and schedules a meeting with the chef right after lunch.

Time for the meeting with the chef: The restaurateur knows that the chef is a good cook and delivers good food cost, but the chef is a pain. The chef kicks and screams every time a change is made. The restaurateur begins by telling the chef that lunch is a problem. Specifically, the labor cost associated with lunch service is too high and the guests are unhappy with the menu selection as well as the time required to eat at the restaurant. The restaurateur asks the chef to develop a lunch menu that can be delivered more quickly and uses less labor, has lower price points, and offers a more casual cuisine. The restaurateur suggests a grilled steak sandwich with roasted onions and an eggplant sandwich with goat cheese and sun-dried tomatoes. As usual, the chef begins to defend her menu, claiming that her staff will quit if lunch becomes more causal and many customers will leave. The restaurateur listens but explains that he wants the new menu to review by tomorrow morning with an implementation timeline attached.

The staff is beginning to set up the dining room for dinner. The restaurant is fully committed tonight with time for only one last meeting. A new hotel is opening across town, and the hotel company wants to discuss the development of a casual version of the restaurant for one of the hotel's dining facilities. The restaurateur likes the idea of a second unit but only if the financial deal is right. However, he can't discuss the opportunity any further because he must race back to the restaurant. It's time for the curtain to go up and dinner service to begin.

31

SETTING UP YOUR BUSINESS FOR SUCCESS

Organize, Organize, Organize

An entrepreneur has many duties. Now that we have competed Phase 1, the entrepreneur must move from deal maker to project manager. To me, Phase 2 is the most difficult. I have the skills to effectively operate in Phase 1 and Phase 3, but my background in Phase 2 is limited. Further, because this book is intended to provide guidance in only Phase 1, Phases 2 and 3 will be addressed as an overview.

PHASE 2: PREOPENING

Preopening can be divided into design/construction, human resources, budgeting, and marketing.

Design and construction require that the entrepreneur understand budgeting and timelines. Each day counts. The designer represents the first major difficulty the entrepreneur encounters in Phase 2. It is nearly impossible to align the incentives of the designer and those of the entrepreneur. The designer wants a calling card. He wants national attention. The more money allocated to the design and buildout, the more likely the designer will win future engagements. Lighting that may or may not have an effect on traffic may bring attention to the designer's work.

Contractors are different; most often they are paid a predetermined fee. They have a small budget for cost overruns, but if they have grossly underestimated what it takes to complete the designer's vision, they will lose money on the job. A good restaurateur will be in touch with the designer and the contractor daily. He will watch every penny. He will verify that the items he has paid for are the items that he is receiving. He will keep track of timelines. He will not leave it up to the designer and the contractor to determine the project's critical path. Whether the issue is permitting or a piece of custom equipment, he will oversee the project at a sufficient level of detail to ensure that the venue is delivered on time and on budget.

Delays in permitting caused one of my early businesses to fail. We expected to open in September but didn't actually open until the following January. We had high fixed costs, so the delay was expensive. Further, our projections counted on Christmas sales to cover cash shortfalls. By the time we opened, we were saddled with debt and didn't have a busy season to save us.

Human resources consist of recruiting, interviewing, hiring, and training. The entrepreneur must prepare his staff while the restaurant is being built. The chef and the cooks are unique to the concept's positioning. For example, a fine-dining restaurant needs a chef and cooks with fine-dining experience. Members of the wait staff, however, have certain traits regardless of the sector where they work. Specifically, a good waitperson will have pride and energy and be extroverted and empathetic. The National Restaurant Association provides outstanding interviews that allow you to identify candidates with those characteristics.

Budgeting in the preopening phase is simple. The critical point in preopening budgeting is to be as frugal as possible because, without a doubt, you'll need that money as working capital.

It is never too early to begin your marketing campaign. Regardless of your positioning, your concept will have two marketing categories: (1) business to consumer and (2) business to business.

Business-to-consumer advertising is that found in consumer magazines and newspapers along with such guerrilla marketing as street teams. Business-to-business advertising is that in business and trade magazines, direct business advertising for corporate functions, and marketing to travel companies like hotels and airlines.

PHASE 3: OPERATIONS

Now the entrepreneur is a restaurateur. The restaurateur has three titles: brand manager, product manager, and chief financial officer.

Together, brand manager, product manager, and chief financial officer equal president. The restaurateur wrote the business plan and acquired the funding. Only the restaurateur can properly manage the brand when the business is in its infancy. Only the restaurateur can determine whether the advertising and the image the ads project are consistent with the menu, décor, location, and service. The restaurateur must be a product manager. He must garner feedback from the guests to determine whether the product is exceeding the guests' expectations. Even in cases where the restaurant has a chef (rather than a cook), the restaurateur should be the one to determine whether the product is appropriate for the brand and to analyze the guests' feedback. In most instances, chefs are not qualified to determine whether the menu is consistent with the overall brand. Further, it has been my experience that most chefs want to cook food that they believe will further their career and not necessarily the food the guests desire.

Last, a restaurateur must understand the numbers. Bookkeepers and accountants can generate financial statements, but as president of the organization, the restaurateur must be capable of interpreting the data. The information a restaurateur garners from financial statements is the basis for decision making. Many aspiring restaurateurs lack the discipline to learn to read financial statements. Restaurateurs at one time operated by feel, but this is a new era with a new breed of entrepreneur entering the restaurant industry. Today's restaurant entrepreneur must understand technology, marketing, finance, accounting, human resources, and operations. Gone are the days when entry into the restaurant industry was a last resort. Today's restaurant entrepreneur selected this industry over many other possibilities.

A *new beginning*

The last 31 chapters are just the beginning. A successful business requires constant education, expert advice, and fearless evaluation. What am I good at? Can I provide the guidance the business requires in its current phase? You now have been exposed to the life of the entrepreneur. To many, the stories in this book will change their mind: "Maybe I don't want to be my own boss; maybe I like having a steady paycheck and time with the family." For a few dedicated individuals, however, the painful stories in this book and the arduous task of establishing the skills required are worth the opportunity to achieve greatness. The book resonates with a unique few who state: "I am not like the rest of them." They are the men and women who will go to any lengths to leave their mark on the world. They are the business leaders of today and the future. Where would we be without the dreams of Bill Gates, Fred Smith, or Chris Sullivan? Maybe it's a restaurant or an environmental testing company or an application service provider or a clothing design and manufacturing firm. It is these fearless few who are willing to take a risk, accept the outcome, and do it all again and again until they achieve their dream. Entrepreneurs are the foundation of our workforce—It's their ventures that provide jobs. Their entrepreneurial dreams become the backbone of communities. They pay for employees' health insurance, broaden and expand families' lifestyles, and set standards for efficiency and productivity that make American business the best in the world.

After reading this book, you have no excuse for entering a business you're not qualified to run. There is no reason you haven't fought for a fair lease with your landlord. There is no reason you haven't attempted to generate a seamless concept and worked to develop a formidable team. As an entrepreneur, you have a tremendous responsibility to yourself, your family, investors, employees, your community, and your industry. These responsibilities cannot be taken lightly. A skill you elect not to develop increases everyone's risk. This is a new day. If you want to lead in today's restaurant industry, you must hold skills far beyond managing food or beverage inventory, cooking, or mixing cocktails. You must garner the skills that will allow you to rightfully assume responsibility for the lives of the stakeholders. In the event you choose not to educate yourself on the many facets of the industry, you are obligated to curb your dream before you fail and put the lives of unwitting employees, landlords, and investors in danger.

I had a longtime friend tell me that he believed smart people were too smart to take the risk necessary to make real money (in his theory, money stood for entrepreneurial risk). Interestingly, he is perhaps the most successful person I know. However, I disagree with his assessment. I believe that he does not understand that the goal is the thrill of the journey, pursuit of a dream, and building greatness—not simply the outcome.

I hope this book has given you an inside look into the deal-making phase of the restaurant industry. With proper planning, restaurants can be extremely exciting and very lucrative for an entrepreneur. The more you understand about deal structure and investment returns, the more likely you are to achieve your entrepreneurial goals.

Share t   e!

Bulk discoun
Discounts start a'
retail price.

Custom pu
Private label a
and logo. Or,
a custom par

Ancillari
Workshop
available c

Dynam
Engagin
and insi

Call Dearborn Trad   665)
          or e-mail trad

Dearborn™
Trade Publishing
A **Kaplan Professional** Company